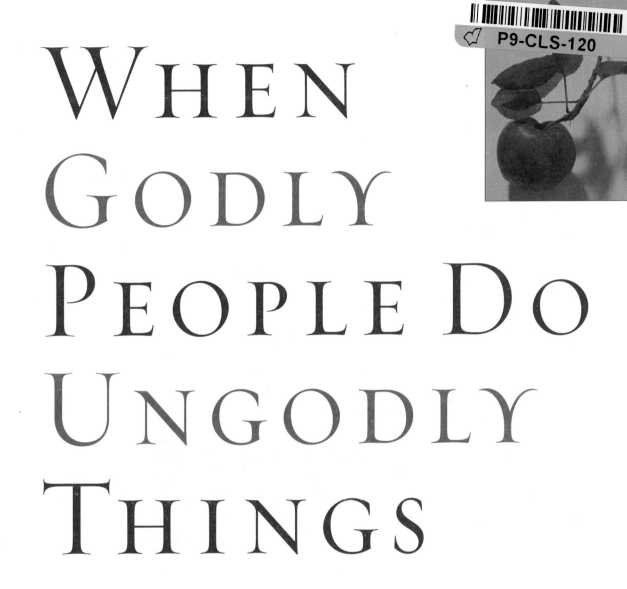

WHEN GODLY PEOPLE DO UNGODLY THINGS

BETH MOORE

LifeWay Press®
Nashville, Tennessee

© Copyright 2003 • LifeWay Press®
Second printing April 2004

No part of this book may be reproduced or transmitted in any form or by any means,
electronic or mechanical, including photocopying and recording, or by any information
storage or retrieval system, except as may be expressly permitted in writing by the publisher.
Requests for permission should be addressed in writing to

LifeWay Press®; One LifeWay Plaza; Nashville, TN 37234-0175.

ISBN 0-6330-9035-2

This book is the text for course CG-0822 in the subject area
Personal Life in the Christian Growth Study Plan.

Dewey Decimal Classification Number: 235.4
Subject Heading: SPIRITUAL WARFARE \ TEMPTATION \ CHRISTIAN LIFE

Editor in Chief: Dale McCleskey
Art Director: Jon Rodda
Editor: Joyce McGregor
Copy Editor: Beth Shive

Cover photo: Howard Bjornson/Photonica
Inside photos: p. 6—Susan Cato; all others—Jon Rodda
Apple illustration: Linda Holt Ayriss, Artville

Unless otherwise indicated, Scripture quotations are from the Holy Bible,
New International Version, copyright © 1973, 1978, 1984 by International Bible Society.

Scripture quotations identified KJV are from the King James Version.

Scripture quotations identified AMP are from The Amplified New Testament
© The Lockman Foundation 1954, 1958, 1987. Used by permission.

Scripture quotations identified NASB are from the NEW AMERICAN STANDARD BIBLE,
© Copyright The Lockman Foundation, 1960, 1962, 1963, 1968, 1971, 1972, 1973, 1975, 1977, 1995.
Used by permission.

Scripture quotations identified CEV are from the Contemporary English Version
Copyright © 1991, 1992, 1995 American Bible Society. Used by permission.

Scripture quotations identified HCSB are from the Holman Christian Standard Bible®
© Copyright 2001 Holman Bible Publishers, Nashville, TN. All rights reserved.

To order additional copies of this resource: WRITE LifeWay Church Resources Customer Service;
One LifeWay Plaza; Nashville, TN 37234-0013; FAX (615) 251-5933;
PHONE (800) 458-2772; E-MAIL to customerservice@lifeway.com; ORDER ONLINE at www.lifeway.com;
or VISIT the LifeWay Christian Store serving you.

Printed in the United States of America

Leadership and Adult Publishing
LifeWay Church Resources
One LifeWay Plaza
Nashville, TN 37234-0175

To L. L.

You have been an unspeakable inspiration—
especially at times when I've grieved while a few others
refused to go the distance and let their Redeemer redeem.
What needless defeat!
I am so proud of you. Can you imagine how He must feel?
A great harvest awaits you, Dear One.
I can't wait to look over your shoulder and celebrate!

BETH MOORE

God captured Beth Moore's heart at a very young age. Her first love was a man with long dark hair, tan and weathered skin, and loving eyes. When she saw a picture of His face tacked onto the wall in Sunday school, she knew Jesus would be the love of her life. Like many children brought up in church, she learned about the Bible, His love letter to her, and sang the familiar children's song, "The B-i-b-l-e, yes that's the book for me! I stand upon the Word of God, the B-i-b-l-e." Beth's love for Jesus Christ grew over the years and at the age of 18 she committed her entire life to be about the things of God.

Beth finished her degree at Southwest Texas State University, where she fell in love with Keith. After they married in December 1978, God added daughters Amanda and Melissa to their household.

As if putting together puzzle pieces one at a time, God filled Beth's path with supportive persons who saw something in her she could not. God used individuals like Marge Caldwell, John Bisagno, and Jeannette Cliff George to help Beth discover gifts of speaking, teaching, and writing. Seventeen years after her first speaking engagement, those gifts have spread all over the nation. Her joy and excitement in Christ are contagious; her deep love for the Savior, obvious; her style of speaking, electric.

Beth's ministry is grounded in and fueled by her service at her home fellowship, First Baptist Church, Houston, Texas, where she serves on the pastor's council and teaches a large Sunday School class. Beth believes that her calling is Bible literacy: guiding believers to love and live God's Word.

Beth loves the Lord, loves to laugh, and loves to be with His people. Her life is full of activity, but one commitment remains constant: counting all things but loss for the excellence of knowing Christ Jesus, the Lord (see Phil. 3:8).

The Lord now uses Beth Moore to encourage women through her Bible studies and conferences to not only stand on the Word of God, but to know what it says. Beth began speaking at local women's luncheons and retreats over 20 years ago. God was faithful to allow her ministry to grow up at the same pace as her family. By the time her two daughters were in middle school, Beth was writing full time and speaking all over the United States. In 1995 the Lord led her to establish Living Proof Ministries to guide women to love and live on God's Word.

Beth and her husband, Keith, will soon celebrate their 25th wedding anniversary. Last summer they traveled to Africa to minister to missionaries and to fulfill Keith's life-long dream of hunting on a safari. Their two daughters and son-in-law are all involved in ministry. Amanda works at Living Proof and Melissa is earning a Biblical studies degree at Moody Bible Institute in Chicago.

Beth's previous Bible studies have explored the lives of Moses, David, Paul, Isaiah, Jesus, and John. In this study of *When Godly People Do Ungodly Things* she invites you along as we learn Satan's strategy for destroying the testimony of Christians and how to arm ourselves against his attacks. May you be blessed by your journey, as were those who traveled to Jackson Hole, Wyoming, for the videotaping and those who worked with Beth to bring you *When Godly People Do Ungodly Things*.

CONTENTS

FOREWORD

When Beth and I first met several years ago, it didn't take us long to become deeply engrossed in conversation. Our discussions were lively and energizing. They never were boring but neither were they very personal. We knew we both had an avid interest in helping people live in truth. After all, Beth was a Bible teacher and I was a therapist working with a Christian psychologist and seeing more Christian castaway church members than I cared to acknowledge. Clearly, we agreed, Satan was lying to our sisters and brothers and many were falling prey to his devices on a regular basis.

I don't remember at what point in our relationship that it became obvious that separately and prior to when we met, we both had been Had. We had experienced the seduction of the enemy up close and personal in our own lives, and we both had been horrified by it. We never talked specifics. We didn't need to. We just had "a knowing" that explained the passion we shared for the subject. When you have been Had and have found your way back, your heart's desire is that others would find their way back, as well. That is why I was so thrilled to learn that my friend Beth was writing *When Godly People Do Ungodly Things*. I was so aware that the need was great and I knew her passion for God's truth was greater. This was a topic she could not avoid. This was a book she had to write.

In this powerfully effective work, Beth has trumped some of Satan's most damaging lies with God's unalterable truth that there is a way back. His godly ones will not be lost without hope. Repentance, redemption, and restoration are available to His beloved.

Granted, there are those in the faith who believe that if you sin, you are removed from the list of those God uses.

You have taken the grace of God too far. You have proven yourself unfaithful. You have shamed your Father. You have brought disgrace on your elder Brother. You have blown it now and forever more! You are done. Because you have 'been had,' you have forfeited your right to a fulfilled life and ministry as a believer.

Those voices have held sway for a long time with little sound teaching to counteract their reasoning. In her straightforward, inimitable style, Beth has uncovered the major flaw in that way of thinking. It is this: people want to be seduced by the evil one. There is nothing further from the truth. No one in their right mind wants the pain and insult that the seduction of the evil one incurs. Christian people, who know and love God, don't go looking for that kind of punishment.

Beth lays out a clear, understandable, supported case for offering hope to godly people who find themselves seduced by the enemy. I believe this work is a godsend for our age. I recommend it without reservation to all serious Christians, whether or not you believe godly people can do ungodly things. Give this study a chance to raise your awareness of the 'stuff' that is going on around us in these days. Take to heart the Scripture that says, "Be self-controlled and alert. Your enemy the devil prowls around like a roaring lion looking for someone to devour" (1 Pet. 5:8).

May you be blessed beyond measure as you find hope and healing in *When Godly People Do Ungodly Things*.

Jan Silvious lives in Chattanooga, Tennessee. She is the author of *Foolproofing Your Life* and *Please Don't Say You Need Me*.

INTRODUCTION

This Bible study represents one of the most unique writing experiences I've ever had with God. Unbeknownst to me, He's been writing each chapter on my heart for several years. When the message for this book was complete (in His estimation—not mine!), God compelled me to ink it on paper with a force of the Holy Spirit unparalleled in my experience. He whisked me to the mountains of Wyoming where I entered solitary confinement with Him, and in only a few short weeks, I wrote the last line. My most overwhelming emotion at this point is relief. My soul is at rest. I have done to the best of my understanding what God seemed to require of me with a relentless passion.

On behalf of all authors who seek the sole leadership of the Holy Spirit, please allow me to say that we don't just pick and choose our subject matter. In fact, sometimes God assigns us a message that is more radical than we'd choose to be and requires more transparency than we'd ever want to invite! I am being as honest as I know how to be when I say that I did not write these pages by simple preference. I wrote them because had I not, the rocks in my yard would have cried out. What God does with what He's required is His business. I entrust this message entirely to the One who delivered it while I sat bug-eyed.

Certainly I'm not audaciously implying that this book is written under the same kind of divine inspiration as the Holy Scriptures! The Word of God is our only volume of pure truth. We mortals no doubt taint everything we touch however accidentally. What I'm saying is that I wrote this message to the best of my ability under the guidance of the Holy Spirit, and I do not believe it conceptually departs from the precepts of God's Word. I may unknowingly err in interpretation or application, but the overall message of warning, redemption, and restoration are consistent with a God so merciful and courageous, He would dare use a pauper like me.

The only other of my manuscripts Satan tried as hard to hinder or destroy was *Breaking Free*. He hates to let go of a captive. He also hates being exposed as the fraud he is and that's one of the chief goals of this book. My specific prayer for this message is threefold:

- that God will use the pages of this book to shed light on Satan's massive campaign, in our current and future generations, to seduce the saints.
- that God will use this message to remind a battered and bruised believer how loved he is and how much the Father longs for his complete restoration. We have never gone so far that we can't come home. Oh, thank You, Lord!
- that many readers will wise up to Satan's seductive schemes and fortify their lives before he traps them into something ungodly.

This book is written in three parts. Part 1 is the warning, both biblical and experiential, that Satan is heightening his attack on those who are devout believers in Jesus Christ. Part 2 comprises ways we can fortify ourselves against Satan's full-scale attack on the lives of the elect in the latter days. Part 3 is the road home for the one who has been deceived and seduced by the enemy into a season of ungodliness.

When Godly People Do Ungodly Things would never have been written without the vigilant prayer and fasting of a thousand prayer warriors who built a firewall fortress around me for several weeks. I am unspeakably humbled by their around-the-clock provision of prayer protection. Many took "hits" on my behalf that can only be explained as spiritual warfare. I am astonished and deeply indebted to them for their willingness to war so faithfully on behalf of this message. They enabled me to write while entirely alone many miles from home without experiencing a single hint of oppression. Satan was utterly defeated.

One of the peculiarities about this assignment is that God also required me to fast. He would not release me to eat until the very end of each day after all writing for that day was accomplished. Sometimes He would not release me until the end of the next day. Never before has He asked me to do such a thing while writing a book. Many authors may fast in advance of a project, but we feel we need the brain food during the actual process. This time God would not permit any such approach. To tell you how adamant He was, the one time I thought I'd be fine to eat breakfast; my thoughts became completely warbled and confused until midafternoon. This message's requirements were so unusual and intriguing to me that I couldn't help wondering why. Finally God gave me understanding and I realized that He was applying the principle Christ introduced in Mark 9:29 (KJV). This book—written specifically to expose one of the most insidious assaults of the evil one—would "come forth by nothing, but by prayer and fasting."

What God required of a thousand prayer warriors and me gave us just a hint how much the enemy was raging against us in the heavenlies.

Once again I find my insecure self wanting to issue some kind of disclaimer about my mental and spiritual health. I really am a pretty normal person. I think. I can tease with the best of them and can take a joke. If it's funny. I am a regular wife and mom. (And does anyone happen to remember that one of the last books I wrote was a sweet, inoffensive mommy book?) I love dogs, and I really like chocolate malts. I am a maniac for Mexican food. I like long Sunday afternoon naps and digging in my flowerbed. Some of my neighbors don't even run in the house when I'm out in the front yard. I'm just your average girl, for heaven's sake!

I didn't ask to write some of the kinds of messages God has appointed me. Believe me, some of the works God has assigned me have not been without sacrifice. My mother went to her grave wondering why I couldn't "just be funny" like I "used to be." Although I certainly received her love, I never received her blessing for the turn my ministry took toward freedom for the captives. Choosing God's approval over hers was a monumental test for me. She's not the only one who liked me better when I did everything far safer. Some of my deeply loved fellow Baptists probably wonder from time to time why I have to be so edgy while brothers and sisters at the other end of the spectrum just wish I'd go ahead and jump off the edge with them. I'm not going to. I cannot write to please man as much as I'd like to at times. So, when you've worked through the last lesson, if you're not pleased, kindly consider telling God and not me. My self-esteem is shakier than His.

Lastly, I want you to know how honored I am to serve you no matter who you are or where you've been. You are a lavishly loved child of God. I humble myself before you and even now have come to my knees in your behalf where I'd like to pray for you.

Father, I am so grateful for the opportunity to serve this brother or sister in the faith. I readily and willingly esteem Your child as better than myself. I do not wish to lord authority over a single one. I wish to serve at the feet of any who will allow me the privilege. How I pray that Your words will fall powerfully upon this child and that mine will be forgotten. I echo the petition I've prayed throughout this journey that You would not let me lead a single one in error. If I have unknowingly left something in this manuscript that is not of You, I beg Your forgiveness, and I pray his or her mind will not absorb it. I pray that You will give Your child ears to hear, eyes to see, and a mind to conceive every word of Yours in this message. Help my brother or sister to approach these concepts with transparency before You. Even if he or she is reading this book in someone else's behalf, I pray each reader will hear You speak straight to his own heart. In Jesus' name I bind the attempt of the enemy to cause any desperate reader to grow an attachment to me rather than You. You are our only salvation. God forbid that any flesh glory in Your presence. You are the only One worthy of a second thought.

You are the love of my life, Jesus. I want others to love You with absolute abandon. Steal our hearts, Lord Jesus, and consume our minds with Your truth. We are otherwise dreadfully at risk of seduction. Expose Your child's vicious enemy and any ground he or she has unknowingly surrendered to him. Rise to Your feet and fight on behalf of Your beloved child, Mighty Warrior. Redeem every single hit and every single hurt caused by the enemy of souls. Cause each precious reader to see this journey to its completion. You will be faithful to finish what You start in each one. I thank You in advance that none who allow Your Word to abide will ever be unchanged. In the powerful, life-giving name of my Deliverer and Redeemer, Jesus, Amen.

Video Response Sheet

INTRODUCTORY GROUP SESSION

IN THE BEGINNING…

1. We are the _____ there was ever a _____.

2. We were _____ out of the _____ _____ of God.

3. We were created out of _____, for _____.

4. LORD God is the _____ name of God.

5. Man was created from the _____ of God.

6. We are made to _____ God in the garden that He has _____ for us,

   and we are not _____ till we do.

7. All _____ begins with "I will." All _____ to God begins with "Thy will."

8. _____ exists because we are the _____ of God.

9. " 'Whoever touches _____ touches the _____ of His eye' " (Zech. 2:8).

10. The only _____ for our war is that we are the _____ of God.

9

WEEK ONE
THE WARNING

I hope you take part in weekly small-groups, video presentations, and discussions. If not, you can work through this study by yourself. However, the accountability, encouragement, and shared experiences of a small group create an ideal learning process.

The Principle Questions will guide your discovery in the Word each week. Each day also provides a Personal Discussion Question (designated by an apple in the margin) that you will apply to your life and discuss with your group.

PRINCIPAL QUESTIONS

Day 1: What does 2 Corinthians 11:3 say Paul feared for the Christians of his day?

Day 2: What does Luke 10:18 suggest about Satan's present power?

Day 3: According to 2 Timothy 2:26, what is Satan's objective?

Day 4: What does Hebrews 10:24-25 tell believers to do?

Day 5: According to 1 John 5:18, how would you explain the difference between Satan's being able to attack us and not being able to grasp us?

1 PRIME TARGETS

I am afraid that just as Eve was deceived by the serpent's cunning, your minds may somehow be led astray from your sincere and pure devotion to Christ.
—2 Corinthians 11:3

A strange thing began to happen soon after my books, *Breaking Free* and *Praying God's Word,* were released. Probably because I admit to such a flawed and sinful past, letters began stacking on my desk from Christians confessing, often for the very first time, to harrowing rounds of defeat at the hands of the devil.

You may be thinking, *So what else is new? Satan has attacked man since his creation.*

I'd like to suggest that something about this spiritual phenomenon might just have taken demonic assault to a whole new level. In the course of this ministry I've read countless letters, and I have come to discern the difference between blatant accounts of mercifully forgiven rebellion and the testimonials I'm talking about here. Why do you think Satan may be more active today in attacking Christians than ever before?

THREE STREAMS OF EVIDENCE

I need to clearly state that three streams of evidence lead me to believe Satan is on a rampage. As we proceed, I want to ask you to consider the significance of each.

1. A Growing Stack of Testimonies

What has terrified me is the growing stack of letters from believers who loved God and walked with Him faithfully for years then found themselves suddenly overtaken by a tidal wave of temptation and unholy assault. Many believers are convinced such things can't happen. "Not to good Christians." They are wrong. And through the course of this study, I hope to prove it.

How do you react to the statement that Satan especially targets whole-hearted believers?
- ☐ I don't believe it for a minute.
- ☐ Yes, I've seen this in action.
- ☐ I'm not sure.
- ☐ Tell me more.

I am convinced that many accounts of formerly pure lives suddenly knee-deep in the mire are absolutely authentic. Not one of them presents him- or herself as an innocent victim. They are horrified and taken aback at what they have done and what they appear capable of doing. Over and over, I've heard renditions of the statement, "For the life of me, I can't figure out how something like this could have happened."

2. Scripture Supports the Idea

The first stream of evidence is the testimonies of scores of believers. Now let's turn to the second. I don't care how many testimonials I receive, I would not give their suggestion that godly people can suddenly do ungodly things a second thought except that Scripture completely supports the idea.

> Read 2 Corinthians 11:3 in the margin. Underline what Paul feared for the Christians of his day.

I am fearful, lest that even as the serpent beguiled Eve by his cunning, so your minds may be corrupted and seduced from wholehearted and sincere and pure devotion to Christ.
—2 Corinthians 11:3, AMP

> What kind of person does Paul seem to describe in these verses?
> - ☐ A slacker Christian
> - ☐ A carnal believer
> - ☐ Someone who has failed to grow in Christ
> - ☐ Someone seriously dedicated to Christ

Wholehearted. Sincere. Pure devotion to Christ. That very kind of person can be beguiled by the enemy, whose utmost fantasy is to corrupt and seduce the real thing. Unsettling, isn't it? Let's take a look at another unnerving statement.

> Galatians 6:1 from *The Amplified Bible* appears in the margin. Underline the words that describe those who are spiritual. Circle the danger involved.

Brethren, if any person is overtaken in misconduct or sin of any sort, you who are spiritual [who are responsive to and controlled by the Spirit] should set him right and restore and reinstate him, without any sense of superiority and with all gentleness, keeping an attentive eye on yourself, lest you should be tempted also.
—Galatians 6:1, AMP

Even the one who is spiritual, "responsive to and controlled by the Spirit," can be tempted by the same sins that have overtaken another. One might argue, "Yes, the one who is spiritual might be tempted, but he surely wouldn't fall for it."

> In 1 Corinthians 10:12, who does Paul say is in danger of falling?

_____

Not only can the godly suddenly sprawl into a ditch from a solid, upright path, I believe many do. As the days, weeks, and months blow off the kingdom calendar, I am convinced that the casualties are growing in number by harrowing leaps and bounds. Many just aren't talking because they are scared half to death. Not so much of God as they are of the church. To say that the body of Christ would be shocked to know how bloody and bruised by defeat we are is a gross understatement. Among the better news is that God is most assuredly not shocked. Grieved perhaps, but not shocked. You see, He told us this was coming.

I told you three streams of evidence led me to the conclusions in this study. The first was the testimony of believers who have been seduced into sin. The second is the warning in Scripture that Spirit-filled believers can be overtaken. The third stream of evidence has to do with the end of the age.

3. The End of the Age

In Christ's discourse to His disciples concerning the signs of His coming and the end of the age, He emphatically warned of an increase in deception, lawlessness, and wickedness. Undoubtedly, the New Testament indicates that an ever-increasing wickedness will rise furiously as we approach the second coming of Christ.

Read 2 Thessalonians 2:7-8. Who will be revealed when Jesus returns?

_____

If the apostle Paul could testify in his generation that "the secret power of lawlessness is already at work" (2 Thess. 2:7), who can begin to estimate the acceleration that has taken place over the last two thousand years?

The area of biblical study called *eschatology* deals with the ultimate or last things. Different scholars of wholehearted commitment to Christ disagree over many details of eschatology. Some scholars believe that we either have entered or are about to enter the time of escalating conflict that will usher in the return of Christ—the last days. Other scholars point to evidence that the biblical last days extend from the time of the apostles to the return of Christ. Either way, Beloved, we are living in the time closer than ever before to the end events of Christian history.

Jesus warned His followers of a time of severe persecution, a time of " 'great distress, unequaled from the beginning of the world until now' " (Matt. 24:21).

> We are closer than ever before to the end events of Christian history.

Read Matthew 24:9-12. What five warnings did Jesus give His disciples?

1. _____

2. _____

3. _____

4. _____

5. _____

These warnings of Christ have applied to all ages, but many Bible scholars believe they point specifically to the war going on in our present and near future.

Combined with the evidence of stream one and stream two, I'm convinced we must prepare ourselves to deal with the assault that is here and the one that is coming.

Clearly, we are living in the best of days and the worst of days. While fresh winds of the Spirit are blowing on many of our churches and a double portion of anointing is bestowed on many believers, the Word also strongly suggests that we are occupying planet Earth during the scariest time in human history to date. You need look only as far as your own community to stare 2 Timothy 3:1-5 in the face.

How does Paul describe people in the last days in 2 Timothy 3:1-5?

_____

_____

List some ways you see the relevancy of these Scriptures today.

_____

Perhaps the end of this age is best characterized biblically by the word *escalation*. Christ compared the signs of the end of our present age to birth pains (Matt. 24:8)—an analogy many of us who have given birth understand with startling clarity. With time, the pains grow far more intense and much closer together. I am not remotely an expert in biblical eschatology, but the birth pains for a coming era have vastly increased and intensified, particularly in the last 50 years.

Many argue that every generation of believers since the ascension of Christ has believed itself to be in the last days. While that could be true, no former generation has possessed our satellite and Internet capabilities, which pave the way for a worldwide hookup. No previous generation could boast the astonishing modes of worldwide travel and research capabilities that ours can. The 20th century trotted its way onto the kingdom calendar by horse and buggy, then pushed the speed of light as it waved its way out through cyberspace.

Our present purpose is not to study the mounting statistics of fulfilled prophecy. We want to understand how godly people can do ungodly things. Then we want to search out biblical remedies. So what does the approach of the end have to do with godly people falling before a satanic assault? Everything!

What does Revelation 12:9,12 tell us about Satan's attitude toward the end?

_____

If you and I have reason to be interested in end-time events, imagine what is at stake for Satan! Believe me, he knows every single sign of the end, and he reads them with the panic of one reading his own obituary in advance. The closer the calendar draws to Christ's return and the devil's crushing defeat, the more furious he becomes. Who are the chief targets of Satan's ever-increasing fury? We are.

What do you believe is Satan's motivation for mainly targeting believers?

_____

I believe Satan has two primary motivations: (1) to exact revenge on God by wreaking havoc on His children and (2) to try to incapacitate the believer's God-given ability to overcome him.

Revelation 12:11 says, "They overcame him by the blood of the Lamb and by the word of their testimony." Once we are covered by the blood of the Lamb, like the angel of death during the first Passover night, Satan cannot enter our abode. Those of us who have received Christ as our personal Savior are the dwelling places of the Holy Spirit (1 Cor. 6:19-20). Our doorposts are covered by the precious blood of our Passover Lamb. Neither Satan nor his demons can enter us.

The more we understand what the covering of Christ's blood means to us, the more we overcome a foe who is otherwise far too strong for us. Satan's worst nightmare is being overcome—particularly by measly mortals. He knows the Bible says we overcome our accuser in two primary ways. If he can do nothing about the blood of the Lamb covering the redeemed, what's a devil to do? Go for the word of their testimony! Satan is out to destroy the testimony of the believer in Christ. The more influential the testimony, the better. His murderous eye is on the sparrow, and he doesn't have much time. His strategy is to kill as many birds as possible with one stone.

How does 1 Peter 5:8 define Satan?
☐ A sweet kitty   ☐ A gentle cat   ☐ A roaring lion

What does the verse say Satan seeks to do?

_____

Has Satan ever tried to devour you? ☐ Yes   ☐ No   ☐ Not certain If so, how?

_____

What was Peter's advice in 1 Peter 5:9?

_____

Look back at the final word in verse 9. The word is *sufferings*. I don't know how many times I've repeated the statement I'm about to make, but I'll keep saying it until at least one skeptic hears: Not everyone in a stronghold of sin is having a good time.

Many people who by the grace of God have never been had by the devil wrongly assume that all departures from godliness are nothing but defiance, rebellion, and proofs of inauthenticity. They have no idea of the suffering involved when someone with a genuine heart for God slips from the path.

Tangling with a roaring lion who is trying his hardest to devour you can constitute real and authentic suffering. In fact, I have suffered more at the flesh-ripping paws of the raging lion than anything else.

Now that countless letters, frantic phone calls, and face-to-face testimonies have found their way to my office, I realize I am far from the only true lover of God whom Satan has tried to devour. Although I would never characterize myself as godly, I will tell you that I loved God more than anything on earth at the times of my greatest demonic assault.

I know plenty of others whom I would not hesitate to have called godly, yet they suddenly found themselves the object of an overwhelming assault of ungodliness. Oh yes, it can happen. In fact, I can't help but think Peter's words in 1 Peter 5:9 may apply to our generation like never before. Based on the findings landing on my desk, increasing numbers of dear brothers and sisters throughout the world are undergoing tremendous suffering at the paws of the roaring lion. Some of it comes in an unexpected, overwhelming season of temptation. Not unlike the temptations Satan hurled at Christ, they can vary in type, but one thing is for sure: They are tailor-made to catch the believer off guard. Many sincere believers fall before they even know what hit them.

Dear body of Christ, it's time we put down the popguns of yesteryear's church. Satan is waging a worldwide nuclear war.

Based on your study today, how were your eyes opened to see that you, believer, are one of Satan's prime targets?

_____

_____

Satan's temptations are designed to catch the believer off guard.

2 BACKGROUND ON SATAN

"Now is the time for judgment on this world; now the prince of this world will be driven out." —John 12:31

Many believers have a wrong conception of Satan's power. They think he is somehow parallel to or as powerful as God. Satan is far more powerful, personal, and conniving than many of us thought. Let's be very careful, however, not to dream of giving Satan more credit than he is due. While he is tremendously potent, armed, and dangerous, he is not the equal of the Most High God.

The Lord of hosts maintains authority over all powers and principalities. Satan is merely a created being. That doesn't mean the evil one is not a threat. At our strongest moments we are no match for him. Only the Almighty Three-in-One can overpower Satan. We walk in the victory Christ won for us only when we are "strong in the Lord and in his mighty power" (Eph. 6:10).

A good time has come for a little background check on our enemy.

How did Jesus refer to Satan in John 12:31 and 16:11?

_____

What does Luke 10:18 suggest about Satan's present power?

_____

So why is a defeated enemy so hard at work in a post-Calvary world? Perhaps this illustration will help. As you read the illustration, look for the parallel between how a U.S. president takes office and how Christ will assume His throne.

In the United States our presidential elections occur in November, but the new president does not assume his position until January. Let's see if I can explain the parallel. I believe in a literal reign of Christ on this earth. I am convinced Scripture teaches that Christ Jesus will visibly return to earth and rule in righteousness for a thousand years. I also believe that the "scroll" described in Revelation 5 is somewhat of a title deed to the world system. God permitted that authority to fall into Satan's hands for a time, after man's forced exodus from the garden. One day soon God will place that title deed back in the hands of its rightful ruler. At the God-ordained time, Christ will return to earth, conquer every foe, and take His seat of authority.

We now live in the period leading up to Christ taking His rightful throne. Christ is already Lord of lords and King of kings, but His kingdom is currently not of this world (see John 18:36). The day is coming when the nature of the kingdom will change. The Christ who reigns today in believers will reign outwardly and absolutely. He will take back what the enemy has stolen.

How would you explain to a new believer the idea you just read?

_____

_____

What political term does the illustration suggest could be applied to Satan?

- ☐ Favorite son
- ☐ Lame duck
- ☐ Front runner
- ☐ Shoe in

As if Satan needed any more reason to rage, his situation becomes even more bleak. Not only is he a lame duck but his time is short. Peter described the consummation of the age in these words: "The heavens will disappear with a roar; the elements will be destroyed by fire, and the earth and everything in it will be laid bare. That day will bring about the destruction of the heavens by fire, and the elements will melt in the heat. But in keeping with his promise we are looking forward to a new heaven and a new earth, the home of righteousness" (2 Pet. 3:10,12-13).

Don't miss the significance of Peter's words from Satan's perspective. All beings will be in their eternal state from this time forward—whether redeemed in the presence of God or unredeemed in the lake of fire.

What does Revelation 20:15 tell us about the destiny of many people?

_____

_____

Think soberly of the words, "into the lake of fire." Satan rages—he knows his eternal destiny bears down on him like an approaching freight train, and he is out of options.

The thought of the future of the unredeemed makes me shiver. I have no desire for anyone to go there. Not even the vilest sinner. I pray for all to repent! If God was willing to save me, He is willing to save anyone who asks.

What does the Lord desire according to 2 Peter 3:9?

_____

_____

In my illustration, election day took place on the cross. Christ has the only valid claim as the ultimate ruler of all creation. That's why the apostle John saw "a Lamb, looking as if it had been slain, standing in the center of the throne, encircled by the four living creatures and the elders. ... He came and took the scroll from the right hand of him who sat on the throne" (Rev. 5:6-7).

The one on the throne is God, of course. He is the all-powerful, ultimate ruler of heaven and earth, and nothing happens except by His perfect or permissive will. Yes, Satan has been "prince of this world," but only by divine permissive will and to accomplish God's own purposes. Satan was completely defeated by the offering of the perfect, sinless life of the Son of God on the cross. One day Christ will assume full reign of the world system where Satan has wreaked such havoc. Presently, however, the world exists in the period between the new election and the earthly inauguration of Christ.

Satan was completely defeated by God's offering His perfect, sinless Son on the cross.

Suppose we had a wicked president who knew he had already been defeated in the election and his removal from office was imminent.

How might a wicked president wield and abuse his power in the time he had left?

_____

_____

On a mammoth, incomprehensible scale, I believe that's what we're presently experiencing.

Satan reads the signs of the times like *The Washington Post.* Christ's kingdom is here now and will also be in the future. The archdemon knows his time of trying to undermine it is coming to a close, so he furiously unleashes his power to the full extent of God's permissive will. The dragon is in a tailspin, and he is whipping everything he can in the time he has left. Because his ultimate fury is at God, nothing gives Satan greater unholy pleasure than assaulting God's children. Hence, our present conflict.

Our purpose through this study, then, is to understand how the people described in 2 Corinthians 11:2-3 as being wholeheartedly, sincerely, and purely devoted to Christ can be beguiled by Satan and have their minds corrupted and seduced.

Certainly no one will argue that a believer can be characterized as godly while practicing ungodly things. Our task is to understand how a person who has consistently walked with God can be so powerfully seduced to ungodliness.

If I were forced to put an entire concept in a nutshell, I'd have to say that somewhere along the way, the godly person walked into a well-spun lie. Lies are Satan's stock in trade. He fathers every deception (John 8:44) and seduction (2 Cor. 11:2-3), but he does not personally carry out all of them. Unlike God, Satan is not omnipresent. Satan can only be in one place at a time, but he has a massive number of unholy hosts who carry out his purposes.

How do Psalm 91:11-12 and Hebrews 1:14 describe the ministry of angels?

_____

_____

Angels were never meant to distract us from worshipping God, but their activity in our lives appears biblically legitimate. Keep in mind that Satan is the ultimate counterfeiter. Anything God does, Satan attempts to counterfeit.

What has Satan been doing all along according to Isaiah 14:14?

_____

_____

I would not be at all surprised if Satan counterfeits God's appointment of angels to every believer by appointing demons to every believer. In this way, we all become targets of Satan's temptations and works of destruction, yet not often by Satan himself. Rather, we must usually deal with the demons sent to do his bidding.

The Word of God often refers to demonic spirits as unclean spirits. Here we have a critical clue to Satan's objective in the life of a believer. When we receive Christ, we are

Satan's ultimate fury is at God.

made clean. As far-fetched as this may seem to us at times, the Word of God unashamedly calls the redeemed of Christ *saints* or *holy ones*. Ephesians 5:25-26 tells us that "Christ loved the church and gave himself up for her to make her holy, cleansing her by the washing with water through the word, and to present her to himself as a radiant church, without stain or wrinkle or any other blemish, but holy and blameless."

Has today's lesson given you insight into who Satan is? If so, summarize.

_____

_____

 # 3 SEXUALLY-ORIENTED BONDAGE

Flee from sexual immorality. All other sins a man commits are outside his body, but he who sins sexually sins against his own body. —1 Corinthians 6:18

Please don't think for a moment that all seduction is sexually oriented. Most assuredly it is not. Believers can be seduced by power, money, position, false doctrine, or by any number of flesh-fueling pumps.

However, Satan so vehemently despises what Christ has done for mortals that one of his chief objectives is to make the clean feel unclean. Oh, how he desires to stain the beautiful bride of Christ. Satan can't *make* the bride do anything, so he does everything he can to *get* her to. How is this best accomplished? He tries to corrupt thoughts to manipulate feelings.

Satan knows that the nature of humankind is to act out of how we feel rather than what we know. One of our most important defenses against satanic influence is learning to behave out of what we know is truth rather than what we feel. Satan's desire is to modify human behavior to accomplish his unholy purposes.

According to 2 Timothy 2:26, what is Satan's objective?

_____

If we have received Christ as our Savior, Satan is forced to work from the outside rather than the inside. Thus, he manipulates outside influences to affect the inside decision-makers of the heart and mind.

We have just arrived at the primary reason why one of Satan's most powerful weapons is sexual seduction. Remember, he wants to make the clean feel unclean in hopes that they will act unclean.

Few things accomplish Satan's goal of inducing feelings and actions of uncleanness in those who are clean like sexual seduction. Somehow Satan makes sure it just seems dirtier than the rest of the dirt. He also likes to instigate falls that carry long-term effects.

Sexual sin is a perfect choice to achieve his goals. It can be highly addictive. It breeds shame like nothing else and has uniquely horrendous ramifications.

> Based on 1 Corinthians 6:18-20, why is sexual sin a perfect choice to achieve Satan's goals?

_____

_____

Stealing, like all sin, is serious and carries lasting consequences of violating God's law. Yet if I stole money and then changed my mind and dumped it in the garbage, in some respects I could walk away without taking the sin with me. However, if I commit sexual sin, I have a much harder time dumping the garbage. Why? Because spiritually speaking, it got on me somehow. The sin was against my own body and wields a much stronger staying power.

Sexual sin can be dumped, all right, but not in a garbage bin. Only Christ through the power of His cross can peel off the adhesive effects of sexual sin. The sin against the body somewhat resembles the outer layer of skin on a burn victim. It must be peeled off, and fresh new skin must be allowed to grow. Satan cannot get inside a Christian, but sexual seduction is one of the most powerful ways the fires of hell can burn the outside of a believer. The sin is forgiven the moment the person repents, but healing from the ramifications can take longer.

Brick by brick, God builds a mighty fortress around our lives as we learn to bring to the light (through open dialogue with God) that which we by human nature leave in the dark. Beloved, we must learn to trust God with our sexuality. Fig leaves wouldn't hide Adam and Eve from God, and our modern forms of fig leaves won't protect us from the enemy. Surely it's more than coincidental that Satan is having his greatest field day over the very dimension of our lives that we are most reluctant to bring before God for help, healing, and wholeness.

We discussed the approaching end of the age as a reason for the rising phenomenon of godly people being enticed to do ungodly things. Christ referenced the " 'increase of wickedness' " as one of the signs of the end of the age and His coming (Matt. 24:12). I'm not sure we have any greater evidence that we are entering the latter days than the incomprehensible mushrooming of sexual sin.

> In the following articles, circle the statistics of money spent and the number of porn site users.

According to the cover story of the March 2000 Online U.S. News entitled "A Lust for Profit," "Web surfers spent $970 million on the access to adult-content sites in 1998, according to the research from Datamonitor, and that figure could rise to more than $3 billion by 2003." The article also claims that "with the dot-comming of America near complete, salacious fare remains a huge—and growing—cyberspace draw. According to Neilson NetRatings, 17.5 million surfers visited porn sites from their homes in January [2000], a 40 percent increase compared with four months earlier."[1]

In an article entitled "Devastated by Internet Porn," writer Steve Gallagher of Pure Life Ministries cited an even more troubling statistic. "Tragically, the percentage of Christian men involved is not much different than that of the unsaved. According to a survey of pastors and lay leaders conducted by _Leadership Magazine,_ 62% have regularly viewed pornography."[2]

God forgives sin the moment we repent, but its ramifications can take longer to heal.

What is most alarming to you about these statistics?

_____

_____

As we consider how godly people can be enticed into doing ungodly things, please keep in mind that religious position and godliness are not synonymous. Neither guarantees the other. We can certainly be in church leadership positions without ever having a pure and wholehearted devotion to Christ. The horrible tragedy is how many among those statistics may have formerly lived godly lives.

In 1 Timothy 4:1 Paul made a statement pertinent to our present subject matter: "The [Holy] Spirit distinctly and expressly declares that in latter times some will turn away from the faith, giving attention to deluding and seducing spirits and doctrines that demons teach" (AMP).

Seduction can take many different forms, but Satan is no doubt having an illicit field day by sexually seducing many saints. Do you see what he has done through E-porn? Not nearly enough believers were coming to him for pornography, so he simply brought it to them. Home delivery. As close as the click of a mouse. It's ingenious, really. Pastors and lay leaders who have never in their lives bought an illicit magazine are suddenly falling under a huge wave of temptation to look "just once" at a pornographic Web site.

The number of believers who had never before viewed pornography and then nearly smothered to death under its life-crushing heap is escalating beyond our wildest imaginations. Perhaps out of curiosity. Perhaps out of loneliness. Perhaps to feel passion again. Perhaps as a way to do mentally what many think they would dare not do physically— a very foolish assumption and one that has proved erroneous many times. Satan has gained a gargantuan victory either way. More often than not, "just once" turns into "just twice." Then three times, four times, and a believer who once walked with God in purity has just developed the fiercest addiction of his or her entire life. Everything is affected. The marriage. The children. The workplace. The ministry.

Have you or someone you know been effected by pornography? What were some of the ramifications?

_____

_____

Of course, Satan already knew that. It went exactly as he planned. It doesn't have to keep going his way, though. His ultimate goal is that people follow the seducing spirits so far that they "turn away from the faith" (1 Tim. 4:1, AMP). If this sounds familiar to you and you are beginning to recognize that you have been powerfully seduced into the demonic doctrine of sexual perversion, don't turn away from the faith! Turn back!

Satan will do everything he can to hang on once he gets a foothold in our lives. Don't wait another minute! The longer we wait to cry out for deliverance and to cooperate with God, the tighter the grip grows on the yoke. If Satan has you in chains and you want out, hang in there! The last part of our study is dedicated to your full return and to the return of others, no matter what sort of yoke binds you or them.

I am compelled once again to shout from the rooftops what I've said before: The body of Christ is being sexually assaulted by the devil! We must learn how to defend ourselves in the power of God's Word and His Spirit.

Just as we teach our young daughters how to guard themselves against sexual assaults, the body of Christ has got to be taught how to guard her virginity. Oh, that the church would start dealing openly and honestly with crimes against itself! It's time we dump the denial, pick up the Sword of the Spirit, and learn how to use it.

As you close your study today, would you be willing to pray the following prayer with me? Personalize the prayer by using the pronouns *me, I,* and *my.*

Oh, God, please help us. We are under such attack. Far too many believers who have histories of faithfulness with You are falling for the devil's schemes. Please open our eyes and show us the way! Hear the desperate cries of Your children.

4 COMMON CLAIMS OF THE SEDUCED

"We do not have a high priest who is unable to sympathize with our weaknesses, but we have one who has been tempted in every way, just as we are—yet was without sin. Let us then approach the throne of grace with confidence, so that we may receive mercy and find grace to help us in our time of need."
—Hebrews 4:15-16

I told you on day 1 how my concern grew out of reading a stack of unnerving testimonials from people who had devoted their lives to Christ and walked with God consistently for an extended period of time only to be suddenly seduced into ungodly behavior. I knew I was looking at the very essence of 2 Corinthians 11:2-3. I poured over their stories with great attention and growing alarm, all the while asking God to give me discernment. As I read their stories and reflected on my own, I kept thinking, *Do you know how many Christians don't believe this is possible?*

I have since made a case study of sorts out of many of their experiences. I met with a substantial number of them face-to-face, not as a counselor but as a researcher. I asked some hard questions and got what I believe were some very honest answers.

By no means do I suggest that all seductions share these commonalities. We have no idea how many shapes, sizes, and forms seductions can take. I have been shocked, however, by a number of common claims that I think are worth our notice. I have three reasons I consider exceedingly important to share with you.

1. If you love someone or you're counseling someone who is making similar claims, you need to know that many others have described the same things. Your loved one or your client may not be crazy after all! They may be beguiled!

2. I am hoping and praying with all of my heart that those persons who are presently being seduced and taking this study will use the following claims as a checklist of sorts to help them recognize their seduction. Recognition can be the first sign of light in this dark encounter.

Please don't think for a second that if one or two of these common denominators don't fit that you are not being seduced. I'm certain this list is incomplete and inconclusive. If the majority of these fit, Beloved, you are most likely being seduced. Cry out to God with everything that is in you! Remember, you can't trust your feelings, so if you don't feel like you want to be rescued, reason with yourself and admit that you need to be rescued. Lastly, keep in mind that some of the common claims came in the aftermath of the seduction, so if you are still actively in the stronghold of seduction, you haven't experienced them yet.

3. If you've been through a similar nightmare and have told no one, it's time you had a name for it. Dear one, you've been seduced.

One last reminder before we begin the list. Please remember not to assume that all seduction is sexual in nature. After our last day's homework, you might be inclined to read it into every story. Please think far more widely as you try to grasp the breadth of Satan's expertise. Remember, he's simply after whatever works. Those who were enticed to do ungodly things after living godly lives shared many of the following 16 claims. We will look at them over the next two lessons.

COMMON CLAIMS

1. Individuals were caught off guard by a sudden onslaught of temptation or attack.

Not one planned his or her season of ungodliness. Virtually all of them felt as if they were hit so hard and so fast that their heads were spinning. Many described having already sinned before they even knew what hit them. Sound impossible? Actually, the possibility is stated unapologetically in Scripture. Galatians 6:1 says, "Brothers, if someone is caught in a sin, you who are spiritual should restore him gently. But watch yourself, or you also may be tempted." Concentrate on the word *caught*. One of the definitions of the Greek word *prolambano* describes the sin like this: "catches the individual by surprise, suddenly, without notice, i.e., before he is aware of what has happened."[3] In fact, the *pro* in *prolambano* means "before."

We would not abandon sound theology to say that these kinds of sins can overtake individuals before they realize what is coming against them and put up their guard. Several other versions translate *caught* as "overtaken." After catching his prey off guard, the enemy does all he can to make the victim feel completely trapped; but, as we'll discover, he can't keep up the facade indefinitely.

Have you ever been caught off guard by a sudden onslaught of temptation or attack?

☐ Yes ☐ No ☐ Not certain If so, describe below.

_____

_____

2. The season of overwhelming temptation and seduction often followed huge spiritual markers with God.

These godly people who then did ungodly things were not walking in sin when the wave of seduction hit. I was amazed how many felt they had just entered a new season of growth in their relationships with God—if not a near spiritual euphoria—when the unimaginable happened.

Remember, Christ Himself endured a dreadful time of testing after receiving great blessing. After He was baptized by John, He heard the glorious words from His Father in heaven: " 'This is my Son, whom I love; with him I am well pleased.' " The very next words? "Then Jesus was led by the Spirit into the desert to be tempted by the devil" (Matt. 3:17—4:1). Of course, Jesus endured His season of temptation without sin, but the experience was inconceivably brutal. Knowing all that would come upon us, our faithful God made every provision, even in our temptation.

Have you ever experienced temptation or seduction after a spiritual high?
☐ Yes   ☐ No   ☐ Not certain Explain briefly.

_____

Why do you suppose we are vulnerable at spiritually high times?

_____

_____

3. Everyone described a mental bombardment.

Though we walk in the flesh, we do not war after the flesh: (For the weapons of our warfare are not carnal, but mighty through God to the pulling down of strong holds;) Casting down imaginations, and every high thing that exalteth itself against the knowledge of God, and bringing into captivity every thought to the obedience of Christ.

—2 Corinthians 10:3-5, KJV

Another way to describe the same thing is obsessive thinking. This one isn't hard to understand. Indeed, it is one of the clearest signs of a fierce demonic stronghold.

Remember our key verse? Second Corinthians 11:2-3 specifically states that believers can be devoted to Christ with their whole heart, yet Satan can corrupt and seduce their minds. In the previous chapter of Scripture, Paul had just described a stronghold.

Read 2 Corinthians 10:3-5 in the margin. Underline the descriptive words.

The very nature of a stronghold is that something is exalted in our minds contrary to the knowledge of God. Breaking free from these mentally obsessive strongholds always requires bringing those previously exalted imaginations into the captivity of Christ's authority. No small challenge—one the enemy hopes we're not up to. We have to prove him wrong. We have divine power to demolish strongholds. Only in our own power is the task too much for us.

Have you ever obsessed about something or someone?   ☐ Yes ☐ No ☐ Not sure
How did it affect you?

_____

_____

Do you believe that obsessive thinking can be a stronghold?   ☐ Yes   ☐ No
Why or why not?

_____

_____

4. Many of those caught in relational seductions (not all seductions are relational) testified that Satan got to them through someone close by.

When Satan is trying to wreak havoc on the godly, he isn't always successful with a blatantly ungodly approach. Remember, we're talking seduction here. The nature of seduction implies an unexpected, well-disguised lure. Satan looks for ways he can get close to the godly and gain trust.

The last thing I want to do is suggest that we cease trusting people, but be warned that not everyone who appears trustworthy is. Perhaps we've all had times when we weren't terribly trustworthy ourselves. Again, we should be desperate for discernment. Thankfully, God is willing to supply it. Part of our fortification against seduction will be making sure a door in our lives has not been opened through unhealthy relationships.

God is willing to supply discernment.

Have you ever been caught in a relational seduction? What do you feel lured you into the relationship?

_____

_____

5. Many testified to early warning signals.

Early warning signals are not surprising, of course. The Holy Spirit does not fail to do His job. Over and over I have asked, "Did you ever get a flag of some kind that caused you to think you ought not to proceed in that relationship or situation?" Almost invariably everyone said yes. It came while they were still walking faithfully with God. I asked why they didn't heed the warning, and virtually all of them said they rationalized it away.

Have you ever experienced a situation where you discerned that maybe you ought not proceed, but then you went ahead? Did your poor decisions result in any consequences?

_____

_____

_____

6. Many described their sudden behavioral patterns as totally uncharacteristic.

I can't tell you the number of times I have heard statements like: "I kept thinking, What in the world am I doing? I've never acted like this in my life!" Most mentioned that family, close friends, and associates also noticed uncharacteristic behavior. Anyone who confronted them, however, faced their defensiveness and rationalizations.

Have you ever gone through a season in your life when you exhibited uncharacteristic behavior? Did anyone confront you? How did you respond?

_____

_____

_____

7. Virtually all of them described feelings and practices of isolation.

Satan's temptation of Christ is certainly not the only example of isolation. The Old Testament prophet Elijah fell into a terrible time of depression in isolation after a vivid mountaintop experience with God.

Satan loves isolation. He wants to draw the believer out of healthy relationships into isolated relationships and out of healthy practices into secretive, unhealthy practices. He purposely woos us away from those who might openly recognize the seduction and call his hand on it. Let's beware of anything that separates us from godly people.

What does Hebrews 10:24-25 tell believers to do?

_____

_____

Can you think of someone in your life right now who needs some encouragement? If so, write their initials here. _____ What could you do to encourage them today?

_____

_____

8. Without exception, deception and some level of secrecy were involved.

Remember that the "secret power of lawlessness is already at work" (2 Thess. 2:7). Satan loves secrets and often works through disguises, masquerades, and shrouds. He wants things to stay in the dark because he knows the moment we expose it to the light of God, he's finished.

Deception is an absolute in every stronghold, but the nature of seductive deception is that the lies are often well masked for a while. We are undoubtedly caught in a stronghold of deception when we realize we're starting to "have to lie" to explain our behavior. We reason with ourselves that others just wouldn't understand, but the real reason is that the deceived soon deceive.

Out of the eight common claims that we have studied today, do you relate to any? If so, which ones?
- ☐ Similar claims
- ☐ Recognition
- ☐ Mental bombardment
- ☐ Relational seduction
- ☐ Early warning signals
- ☐ Sudden totally uncharacteristic behavioral patterns
- ☐ Feelings and practices of isolation
- ☐ Deception and some level of secrecy

5 COMMON CLAIMS OF THE SEDUCED, PART 2

*Be self-controlled and alert. Your enemy the devil prowls around like
a roaring lion looking for someone to devour.* —1 Peter 5:8

Yesterday we examined eight common claims of the seduced. Today we'll consider eight more as we continue to see common claims made by people who were enticed to do ungodly things after living godly lives. Remember, this list is given to help you discern whether you are being or have been seduced. Hopefully, you've never been there, but these claims are from scores of believers who have been and who were horrified at what they have done. May these common claims serve as a yellow light flashing: Caution! Believer beware!

9. Many described overwhelming feelings of powerlessness.

The feeling being fueled is a lie, of course, and a perfect example of a doctrine of demons. Believers are only powerless in their own strength, and God has promised to provide a way of escape for every temptation. The power of seduction is indescribable, however—not inescapable or totally irresistible, but indescribable.

If you've never been hit by a satanic tidal wave, you're inclined to think that walking away from any sin is a matter of making a simple decision. You may never have experienced the feeling of being completely overpowered. Again, we see that Satan's attempt is to inspire a feeling so strong that it eclipses the truth.

Have you ever been in a situation in which you felt powerless to do anything?
If so, how did you cope?

_____

_____

The next common denominator could be one major reason why seduction is not easy to walk away from.

10. Many described something we'll call an addictive nature to the seductive sin.

Mind you, they can't fully explain some of the things they felt in the heat of the battle any more than I can explain how I felt in times of my severest warfare. I'm not saying anyone fully understands it. I just asked them to try to describe it. I'm bringing to the table what completely independent sources told—and they didn't know anyone else had said something similar.

What are some things to which people are addicted?

_____

How do you think a person could develop an addiction to seductive sin?

_____

_____

11. Most utterly hated what they were doing.

In all probability, this characteristic is somehow connected to the previous one. Someone extremely dear to me has battled alcoholism for years and is finally winning the battle. She despised what she was doing but felt powerless to stop. The addiction was overwhelming. Similarly, almost every person I interviewed testified that they hated their ungodly behavior but for a season were drawn like a magnet to it. Part of Satan's ploy is to make his victims feel addicted and powerless.

Have you ever felt powerless over a behavior you hate? If so, describe how you felt.

_____

_____

Sometimes the seduction so corrupts the mind and confuses the feelings that it draws off of the pure animal-like instinct of the flesh. The seduced person often deplores what she's doing but in the heat of the battle feels overpowered by it. Sometimes people can describe a time of rebellion with a mischievous grin and even admit to having enjoyed it, but I have never heard a godly person who was seduced by the enemy say they could look back on the time with a smile. All will tell you it was their worst nightmare. It filled their lives with shame, and they ended up being sickened by it.

12. The seduction lasted only for a season.

Needless to say, the time frames vary, but people with a genuine heart for God cannot remain in a practice of sin. At some point they will cry out in total desperation for deliverance. For those who have walked closely with God, the desire for a return to His intimate favor finally exceeds the lure of their seducer. In the end, Satan cannot cut it because he can't sustain it. Those who know the truth will finally recognize the lie.

Write 1 John 3:9 in your own words.

_____

_____

John makes a similar statement in 1 John 5:18, then says something that seems totally to contradict the claims this book is makes: "We know that anyone born of God does not continue to sin; the one who was born of God keeps him safe, and the evil one cannot harm him." *The King James Version* says "that wicked one toucheth him not." I'm not sure either word, *harm* or *touch,* adequately expresses the original. I'm going to let Charles Ryrie explain this one out of his fine work entitled *Basic Theology:* "It means not a superficial touching but a grasping, clinging to, or holding on to someone. Satan can never hang on to the believer with the purpose of harming him, for that believer belongs eternally and irrevocably to God. Satan (or demons) may afflict and even control for a time, but never permanently or eternally."[4]

With this explanation in mind, perhaps *The Amplified Bible* words it best. Read 1 John 5:18 in the margin.

How would you explain the difference between Satan's being able to attack us and not being able to grasp us?

_____

_____

We know [absolutely] that anyone born of God does not [deliberately and knowingly] practice committing sin, but the One Who was begotten of God carefully watches over and protects him [Christ's divine presence within him preserves him against the evil], and the wicked one does not lay hold (get a grip) on him or touch [him].
—1 John 5:18, AMP

Satan cannot possessively lay hold of us, keep us in a grip, or touch us in a way that will utterly destroy us. We may feel destroyed, but we are not. Christ preserves us from Satan's ultimate intent—our total destruction.

The next three common claims of the seduced call for a preface. Like most of you, I prefer to study facts rather than feelings, and I'm aware that we are wavering at times between the objective and the subjective. Let me say something, however, on behalf of many victims of seduction. Each feels as if he or she is the only one in the Christian world who has ever sincerely loved God and then fallen into such uncharacteristic and even horrifying sin.

Because God chose to supply me with so much unsolicited data, I have learned something they may not know: They are not the only ones. Many have been through the same kinds of experiences and have even felt the same inexplicable things. They are not alone and they need to know it. For that reason, I want to share the feelings they described whether or not the reader thinks they are legitimate. I am not asking you to believe them. I am asking you to hear them.

13. Many describe a period of a spiritual numbness of sorts.

Perhaps because they are in such shock and seduction, they often report not feeling the expected feelings of immediate devastation. Many reported that "it just didn't seem real for a while." I'm not sure how Satan does it, but I think he does everything he can to suspend godly sorrow. Why? That's easy! Because godly sorrow brings repentance (2 Cor. 7:10), he wants to delay repentance as long as possible. He keeps his victims so fueled with other confusing feelings that they often report not feeling what was real.

Needless to say, the victim has also resisted the warnings of the Holy Spirit and finally quenched Him enough that the normal spiritual feelings are temporarily diluted. Satan may work enough confusion to be able to delay feelings of repentance for a little while, but he cannot have his way for long. To anyone who has ever truly loved God, those feelings come all right. And when they finally come, the sorrow is almost unbearable.

14. Many used the same peculiar word to describe what they had experienced.

Over and over I have heard the word web coming from those trying to find a word to describe what they felt they had escaped. Keep in mind, they were not aware others were using the same word.

15. Many describe the aftermath as a time of slowly increasing awareness rather than an instant wake up.

I'm aware that I may lose some skeptics here, but I may as well go ahead and get it over with: Many people describe the season following their separation from the seducer like coming out from under the influence of a drug. You may think they were making excuses for their behavior, but by the time most of them contacted me, they had taken full responsibility for their sins and were blaming virtually no one but themselves.

They were not saying the devil made them do it, but they were saying that coming out from under the influence of this very powerful thing they couldn't define was like slowly getting a drug out of their system. The more they woke up, the madder and sadder they became. I am so glad many of you have no idea what these people are talking about. Praise God! At the same time I will tell you that I believe what many are describing is authentic even if I can't adequately explain it.

I know! I know! We want Scriptures, not experientials, and rightly we should. What does 2 Corinthians 11:3 state?

_____

Even those wholeheartedly devoted to Christ can be corrupted and seduced.

This Scripture suggests that even the minds of those who were wholeheartedly devoted to Christ can be corrupted and seduced. I don't think this is entirely unlike a brainwashing of sorts. (With sewer water, I might add.)

I love the wording of *The King James Version* of 2 Corinthians 11:3: "I fear, lest by any means, as the serpent beguiled Eve through his subtility, so your minds should be corrupted from the simplicity that is in Christ." Note the word *simplicity*. In the original language, it means all the things *The Amplified Bible* suggests, but it also indicates the opposite of duplicity. James 1:8 gives a great definition of duplicity: "A double minded man is unstable in all his ways" (KJV).

The simplicity of Christ means we adhere to one ultimate influence. When our minds are opened to the powerful, virtually hypnotic influence of the devil, we are as unstable as a staggering drunk. Just as it requires time for other kinds of toxins to be washed out of our systems, it takes time for the poison the evil one has poured into our minds to drain. We do wake up, however, and boy, are we ever mad.

16. Feelings of devastation and indescribable sorrow finally came, ushering in deep repentance.

This point is critical as we specify the focus of our case study. Nominal or halfhearted Christians may come out of a season of defeat without excessive sorrow, but those who were wholeheartedly, sincerely, and purely devoted to Christ (2 Cor. 11:3, AMP) finally experience such a devastation that they often feel they can't go on.

About now, some readers feel like someone's been reading their mail. You know all too well what I've just described. But how about everyone else? Are you still with me? Please stay with me until the end of our study, even if this section seemed far-fetched.

My dilemma is that I've seen, experienced, and studied too much to totally discount what completely unrelated and perfectly lucid people are saying. I may be thinking outside the lines of my usual belief system, but I do not believe I am thinking outside the lines of God's Word. This I know: God would not let me rest until I told what I've seen. I have never been more certain He sent me forth with a message. I will trust Him with it.

Review the 16 claims that we studied in the last two lessons. Place a check mark by the ones you are struggling with now or have struggled with in the past. If you are not dealing with some of these issues personally, perhaps you know someone who is. Write their initials here and intercede on their behalf.

_____

Next week we will see how a godly person could be vulnerable to the kind of mess we just described.

Video Response Sheet
GROUP SESSION I

1. There are _____ kinds of seduction.

2. Warfare is _____. Seduction is _____.

3. We can be _____, _____, and wholeheartedly _____

   to God and be _____ by the serpent's cunning.

4. _____ turn your _____ on the enemy.

   FOUR CLASSIC ASSAULTS OF THE ENEMY

   A. _____

      God's counteroffer is _____.

   B. _____

      God's counteroffer: Shame is not of _____.

   C. _____

      God's counteroffer: He did not give us a _____ of fear.

   D. _____

      God's counteroffer: The _____ of His authority.

5. The next generation is tired of _____. They want to see _____.

6. God knows where _____ lies. _____ must take responsibility for our sin.

7. We get into a seductive mess by believing a _____.

8. Our ticket to freedom is to look up with an unveiled face before God and say, "_____ _____."

GOD'S PERMISSIVE WILL

Could it be possible for a wholehearted, sincere, and purely devoted follower of Christ to be seduced by Satan? Not only is it possible, it is probable. You've heard the saying, "What you don't know won't hurt you." When it comes to Satan's seductions, trust me, what you don't know *will* hurt you. This week we will discover what makes us targets for seduction and how Satan must seek permission from God before he can attack a believer.

PRINCIPAL QUESTIONS

Day 1: Who does the wicked hunt down according to Psalm 10:2?
Day 2: What did the woman at the well say in John 4:39?
Day 3: In 1 Thessalonians 3:5 and James 1:14, through what two sources are we tempted?
Day 4: How is Job described in Job 1:1?
Day 5: What did Jesus say to Peter in Matthew 16:17-19?

1 SUSCEPTIBLE TO SEDUCTION

This is my prayer: that your love may abound more and more in knowledge and depth of insight, so that you may be able to discern what is best and may be pure and blameless until the day of Christ. —Philippians 1:9-10

We've arrived at a very important place. This week we will consider how a wholeheartedly, sincerely, and purely devoted servant of Jesus Christ could become vulnerable to such powerfully demonic seduction. None of us is ever sinless, but the people we're talking about were not living under the dominion of any sin when they were attacked. No, sin is not where the enemy most often gets his foothold on the godly. Rather, we're about to see, where this kind of victim is concerned, the enemy more often latches on to weakness— or maybe I should say a hidden spot of vulnerability. Of course, Satan knows that weakness can turn to sin in a heartbeat when exposed to just the right amount of pressure.

Who does the wicked hunt down according to Psalm 10:2?
☐ The injured   ☐ The powerful   ☐ The weak

After the case studies I've encountered in the last several years, I have become more and more convinced that victims of seduction share certain vulnerabilities at the time of their attack. Again, I can't imagine that my list includes all points of susceptibility, so be assured up front that I'm far from knowing it all. Furthermore, please do not assume you haven't been seduced just because every shoe doesn't fit.

At this point let me say something very important. If you have never been seduced but share these vulnerabilities, child of God, be warned! You could be headed for the nightmare of your life!

Don't assume you haven't been seduced just because every shoe doesn't fit.

33

Here is my list of the weaknesses that many Christians carry in their hearts, minds, and souls. Please consider them carefully.

1. Ignorance.

Without exception, the number one element that sets believers up for seduction is ignorance! I tried to think of a prettier word, but this is the one the Bible uses. Don't think I mean this as one of my colloquialisms. I am using it in its most literal sense. What we do not know can hurt us!

Throughout the remainder of the list, you will see signs of ignorance—things the seduced did not know. Obviously, one of the most common forms of ignorance was that none of them knew this kind of thing could happen. Read and meditate on each of the following Scriptures:

Hebrews 5:1-2. To whom do the high priests minister? _____

Don't miss the words ignorant, going astray, and weakness. We are at great risk of going astray over ignorance and weakness.

In the margin underline the words in 2 Corinthians 2:11 that Paul was "not ignorant of" (AMP).

To keep Satan from getting the advantage over us; for we are not ignorant of his wiles and intentions.

—2 Corinthians 2:11, AMP

The apostle Paul and his well-educated crew may not have been ignorant of Satan's schemes, but most of us are! We cannot afford such ignorance, particularly as the Day is drawing near (see Heb. 10:25)! We cannot ignore Satan and assume he'll go away. Ignorance flies like a flag over our heads screaming, "Pick me! Pick me!" The apostle Paul repeated over and over, "I would not have you ignorant."

I can't help sharing these last two Scriptures because I have looked back on my times of defeat and cried bitter, angry tears with my own rendition of these verses. What does the writer of Psalm 73:22 say about himself?

_____

Write your own modern update of Agur's confession in Proverbs 30:2-3.

_____

_____

_____

Our next point exposes the area of ignorance that drains our strength faster than any other.

2. Spiritual passion that exceeds biblical knowledge.

With this in mind, let's carefully read 2 Corinthians 11:3: "I am fearful, lest that even as the serpent beguiled Eve by his cunning, so your minds may be corrupted and seduced from wholehearted and sincere and pure devotion to Christ" (AMP). Notice the Scripture talks about the serpent getting to our hearts through our minds. The person described has wholehearted devotion to Christ, but the mind is still vulnerable. Most of ours are too—until we have a horrible scare that teaches us to love God with our whole mind and not just our whole heart. The church in Corinth was passionate but lacked the knowledge to provide a firm, less shakable foundation.

Earlier we highlighted Paul's brief thesis on tearing down strongholds: "Casting down imaginations, and every high thing that exalteth itself against the knowledge of God" (2 Cor. 10:5, KJV).

What are some imaginations or high things that can be exalted against the knowledge of God? Check all that apply:

☐ Reputation   ☐ Pride   ☐ The many ways to heaven
☐ Bible study   ☐ Jesus is the Way, Truth, and Life
☐ The desire for wealth   ☐ Busyness equals godliness

If we don't have the knowledge of God, we are ill-equipped to recognize imaginations that exalt themselves over God. Remember Proverbs 30:2-3? In essence, that's exactly what the writer was saying. We can't just have knowledge about warfare to defeat Satan. We desperately need the knowledge of God, the knowledge of the Holy One! Our only means of getting it is through an intense relationship with God through His Word.

Mind you, I would have told you I had a pretty fair knowledge of Scripture at times of defeat, but in retrospect I knew bits and pieces rather than grasping more of the whole counsel of God. Furthermore, a big difference exists between a head full of knowledge and the words of God literally abiding in us.

On a scale of 1–10, one being little knowledge of God, 10 being the Word alive in you, where would you place yourself?

1	2	3	4	5	6	7	8	9	10

Little knowledge   Word alive in you

Satan strongly desires the destruction of anyone who keeps his or her sword of the Spirit (the Word of God) sharpened by personal use. He knows that weapon becomes dull once the believer's use of Scripture becomes mechanical. Many of those in ministry who fell for seduction had gotten so busy doing the work of God that they slipped away from pure intimacy with God.

Before we move on to the next point, please allow me to offer a word of caution on the other side of this double-edged issue. Yes, spiritual passion exceeding biblical knowledge is a definite weakness, and so is the opposite condition. Please beware! A head full of biblical knowledge without a heart passionately in love with Christ is terribly dangerous—a stronghold waiting to happen. The head is full, but the heart and soul are still unsatisfied. Satan knows that we all long for passion. If we are not given to godly passion, we will be tempted by counterfeits.

Completely passionate and biblically knowledgeable! Oh, God, make us both!

Can you think of a time in your life when spiritual passion exceeded biblical knowledge? ☐ Yes   ☐ No   ☐ Not certain   If so, what were the results?

_____

_____

_____

We've seen two weaknesses Christians carry: ignorance and spiritual passion exceeding biblical knowledge. Now let's turn to a third vulnerability.

3. A lack of discernment.

Discernment means to see or understand the difference. I am convinced that discernment will be one of the most important criteria in the devoted believer's life to provide protection from seduction. Most victims of seduction have not had a history of particularly great discernment.

What does each of the following verses have to say about discernment?

Proverbs 14:33 _____

Proverbs 19:25 _____

Proverbs 28:11 _____

Philippians 1:9-10 _____

Discernment is critical. Do you see how susceptible any of us can be to seduction without it? Celebrate the fact that God honors the heartfelt petition for discernment and will graciously give it and more.

Read 1 Kings 3:9-13. What was Solomon's request?
- ☐ A long life
- ☐ Lots of money
- ☐ A new house
- ☐ A discerning heart

How did God react to Solomon's request?
- ☐ With anger
- ☐ Refused to grant his request
- ☐ Made him beg
- ☐ Promised to give him a wise and discerning heart and more

We need godly discernment to distinguish right from wrong.

Don't miss the fact that Solomon was already wise enough to know that sometimes right and wrong can be difficult to distinguish. He needed discernment and so do we. In our next vulnerability, we will see a kind of discernment we don't often consider.

4. A lack of self-discernment.

This one is so important! We'll let David, a man who certainly fell into sin after godliness, introduce it to us through his very private prayer.

What question did David ask in Psalm 19:12-13?

_____

_____

What request did he make?

_____

_____

What would be the result?

_____

_____

In this particular verse, the Hebrew word translated "error" is *segihah*. According to *The Hebrew-Greek Key Study Bible,* it means "error, transgression, sin committed inadvertently."[1] It stands in contrast to the psalmist's petition for God to keep him also from willful sins. We commit some sins willfully and presumptuously. We commit others inadvertently. The former flows from rebellion and the latter from error, ignorance, and weakness. Again, it's all sin, but we need to distinguish that rebellion is not the only way to get into trouble.

Rebellion is not the only way to get into trouble.

> In the list below, place a "W" beside sins that you would call "willful", and an "I" by sins you would call "inadvertent."
>
> ____ Gossip   ____ Not witnessing   ____ Losing my temper
> ____ Lying   ____ Anger   ____ Immorality
> ____ Greed   ____ Jealousy   ____ Not believing God
> ____ Not caring for the poor and hungry   ____ Reacting wrongly to situations

The word *segihah* comes from the word *sagah*. Hang on to your hat while I tell you what this word means in all its different applications.

"*Sagah:* to waver, wander, go astray ([Ezek.] 34:6); to lead astray (Job 12:16), misdirect (the blind [Deut.] 27:18), seduce; to sin through ignorance, transgress inadvertently ([1 Sam.] 26:21); to reel (as if intoxicated [Prov.] 20:1; [Isa.] 28:7). Evil habits ([Prov.] 20:1; [Isa.] 28:7), immorality ([Prov.] 5:20), and spiritual weakness ([Prov.] 19:27) cause individuals to stray away from God's commands ([Ps.] 119:21,118), much like sheep gradually stray from their shepherd ([Ezek.] 34:6). *Sagah* is also used with reference to a man intoxicated with love ([Prov.] 5:19,20)."[2]

A couple of things greatly interest me here. Keep in mind that the original word for *errors* in Psalm 19:12 comes from this word. These definitions show the close relationship between ignorance, spiritual weakness, and going astray. I also find the references to "reel (as if intoxicated)" and "intoxicated with love" very interesting in terms of our study. More than anything, I hope you didn't miss the sudden appearance of the word *seduce*. I believe the implication could be twofold:

First, our weaknesses and areas of ignorance are huge vulnerabilities to seduction, which can quickly lead to sins committed inadvertently.

I also see a second possible implication. We know that Satan's seduction is purposeful, scheming, and utterly intended for evil. It is well planned and timed; nothing about it is accidental or coincidental. In such cases, are the mortals he chooses to use as the agents of seduction always evil, malicious, and completely intentional?

> Let's see what Scripture implies on the subject. According to Scripture, Satan uses several types of humans in his seductive schemes. We find one type in 1 Timothy 4:1-2.
>
> What does Paul say some will do (1 Tim. 4:1)?
>
> _____
>
> What happens to those who follow deceiving spirits (v. 2)?
>
> _____

Paul presented pretty scathing indictment against those who are such willing servants of Satan's seductions!

Read 2 Timothy 3:1-7. This passage also addresses those the enemy can powerfully use to seduce others. Would you characterize these targets as:

☐ Wholeheartedly devoted to God   ☐ Caught in a trap
☐ Loaded down with sins   ☐ Wise beyond their years

Needless to say, anytime we are loaded down with sins, we are game for seduction.

Look back at the definition of *sagah* one more time. Part of the definition reads: "seduce; to sin through ignorance, transgress inadvertently." Could it be that some Satan uses as puppets or agents for seduction did not willfully and presumptuously volunteer for the job? Could it be that sometimes Satan's mortal agents of seduction have themselves been seduced? I think so. In fact, the seduced may become seducers if they fail to let God radically deal with them through and through.

We are vastly helped when we recognize our own errors, our own transgressions, and the ways in which we've committed sins inadvertently. We are so quick to acknowledge the errors of others, but one of our best defenses is to recognize where we've each gone wrong and where our personal weak places are. We've got to replace our self-condemnation with self-discernment! Lord, help us!

Lord, help us develop self-discernment.

2   TRUSTING GOD WITH OUR PAST

If you, O LORD, kept a record of sins, O Lord, who could stand? But with you there is forgiveness; therefore you are feared. —Psalm 130:3-4

In our previous lesson, we discussed four areas of weakness that make us vulnerable. Today I want us to examine another cause of vulnerability. We need to deal with weaknesses caused by exposure to or experience with false worship or depravity in the past.

I am convinced that one reason the apostle Paul was so worried about the Corinthian church is because they had been exposed to so much false worship and depravity. Indeed, many of them had come directly from those practices. They had fallen for such false teaching in the past that he feared they could be had again: "you put up with it easily enough" (2 Cor. 11:4). Not only that, they were still surrounded by ungodliness in their attempts to live godly lives.

Corinth was vile even by our standards today. Not unlike us, they were constantly exposed to the worship of false idols, sexual looseness, and nudity. Their exposure was literal (right in the street or on the temple grounds as perverted worship); ours is often through billboards, magazine covers, television shows and, perhaps even worse, commercials! Of course the seeker of pornography could tap into endless resources, but we don't have to go nearly that far to be susceptible to seduction.

Any level of exposure can open a door in the mind that Satan might one day decide to use for his advantage. Some of us were exposed to things we should never have seen as children. We don't have to want to be exposed to be exposed. For instance, being exposed to pornography can take a profound toll on the later life, and Satan often makes sure it does. I've heard people talk about finding pornographic magazines in their fathers' things when they were young, then dismiss it as unimportant. Such a discovery frequently has a huge effect on that life and gives Satan a trump card for later.

How do you think billboards, magazine covers, television shows, commercials, movies, or songs make us susceptible to seduction? Plan to discuss this in your group this week.

_____

_____

_____

Can you think of a time when exposure to any of the things you listed influenced your choices? ☐ Yes   ☐ No   ☐ Not certain If so, describe briefly.

_____

_____

_____

Needless to say, experience can open an even wider door than exposure. Satan would be foolish not to try to exploit our past experiences. How many people have come to salvation in Jesus Christ and been forgiven and made new only for Satan to continue to taunt, accuse, remind, and tempt them with past memories of sinful activities? God keeps no record of believers' wrongs, but you can be sure Satan does. He's a meticulous note taker. We've got to start believing God's press about us and not the devil's.

We have such unbelief concerning our new identities in Christ that we practically let Satan get away with murder—the murder of a new self-concept defined in the Word of God. We have raised the question, "Can anyone be seduced?" I still maintain that while it is possible, for some it is less likely. I have the privilege of writing for the same publisher as Henry Blackaby and T. W. Hunt, two men whose shoes I don't consider myself worthy to shine. We know that Satan despises any teacher who dares to instruct believers how to use the Sword of the Spirit. He would do anything he could to destroy any of us. If Satan were to survey Dr. Blackaby, Dr. Hunt, and Beth Moore, looking for someone to seduce, who would be his more susceptible or vulnerable candidate? Hands down, someone more like me! Both of those fine men have led pure lives with very little exposure to or experience with wickedness. They have long track records of faithfulness. Thankfully, by the time I started writing alongside those two fine men, God had taught me volumes, and I was no longer easy prey. I've even learned how to punch the devil back. Still, I will always have to be on guard because I have a past other less-vulnerable believers don't share.

I urge you to do the activity at the top of page 40, but please feel free to make notes in a separate notebook to protect your privacy. You will not be asked to share your response in your Bible-study group.

We've got to start believing God about us.

Either as a child or an adult, what events or experiences do you have in your past that Satan has or might use to seduce you? Add to my suggestions as necessary.

☐ Abuse when you were a child
☐ Parents who did not know how to show love in a form you needed
☐ Death of parent(s)
☐ Divorce in home
☐ Chronic illness of parent
☐ Favoritism among siblings
☐ Rape whether as a child or adult
☐ Lack of Christian discipleship
☐ Marriage to an abusive spouse
☐ Addiction or some drug or behavior
☐ Performance based self-worth
☐ Other _____

Please do some journaling about how these elements of your background have (1) created vulnerabilities in your life and (2) created additional opportunities for you to minister to others.

Dear one, if we don't let God deal with every part of our pasts, our hurts, our secrets, our errors in judgment, our mistakes, our sins, or the handicaps in our backgrounds, any one of them can be like a hibernating bear. Satan, the prowling lion, stalks the mouth of the cave, waiting for just the "right" season. He opens his jaws and lets out a roar so ferocious that the heavens tremble. Only mortals cannot hear the lion roar. The bear stirs. The roars continue. The bear resurrects from its deathlike slumber, rises to its feet, and realizes he is ravenous. The lion hides and watches while the bear eats you alive.

If the description in the last paragraph rings a bell for you, how does it feel when the bear awakens?

_____

_____

Beloved, listen to me carefully. Satan plays hardball. The psalmist testified about his foes and his powerful enemy with the words, "They confronted me in the day of my disaster" (Ps. 18:18). Somehow we secretly hope the devil, as low as he is, surely has enough scruples to draw the line where the fight would be totally unfair, but Satan has no scruples! When we have a disaster, we can count on his being right there confronting us at our weakest, most vulnerable point.

Would Satan take advantage of a helpless child? Yes! Would he descend on the life of a grieving mother? Without question! Would he capitalize on a past we've tried so hard to put behind us? Count on it! We can't just put our pasts behind us. We've got to put our pasts in front of God. Satan is inconceivably mean and will take advantage of any unfinished business.

If you're like I used to be, you might be in a pout about now, thinking, *But it's not fair that my past makes me more vulnerable! We can't do anything about our pasts!* Oh, Beloved, if that last statement is not one of the deadliest doctrines of demons, I don't know what is! Don't you see? The very thing Satan used against me was precisely that I had not done anything about my past! Yes, we can do something about our pasts. We can take them to Jesus! We can't forget them or ignore them. We need Him to take full authority over them so they are no longer a playground for the enemy. Jesus is our Alpha and our Omega. He has been there from our beginning and will be faithful to us until the end. He longs to reframe our pasts and let us see them against the backdrop of His glory. Never ever forget that our God is a redeemer.

In the song of ascent (Ps. 130:3-4,7) below, replace the word *Israel* in verse 7 with your name.

"If you, O LORD, kept a record of sins,
    O LORD, who could stand?
But with you there is forgiveness;
    therefore you are feared.
O _____, put your hope in the LORD,
    for with the LORD is unfailing love
    and with him is full redemption."

Dear one, let Him redeem it! Every bit of your past! Not just the injustices but the blatant sins. Not just the accidental ones but the willful ones! And not just our sins, but our excruciating losses.

God never abuses His authority. He also never shames. Do you remember the woman at the well? After her encounter with Jesus, she ran into town telling about her experience with Jesus.

What did the woman at the well say in John 4:39?

_____

She wasn't ashamed! Do you know why? Because when Christ takes authority over our pasts and we allow Him to confront them, treat them, and heal them, we exchange our shame for dignity! I'm ready to shout hallelujah!

On day 1, we discussed that when Satan targets a believer who has wholehearted, sincere, and pure devotion to Christ, he latches on to weakness more often than sin. You may be wondering, *But what about the sins of our pasts?* Beloved, one of the times when Satan pounced on me most ferociously and used my past sins against me, I had already repented of those sins. They could no longer be used as sins against me. But here's the catch: they were still weaknesses! Why? Because I had asked God to forgive me, but I had never asked God to heal me completely, redeem my past, restore my life, sanctify me entirely, and help me to forgive myself. Until I allowed God to take full authority over them in every way, my past sins—though turned from and forgiven—were still vulnerabilities where Satan could prey.

Thank goodness, my past sins aren't invitations to Satan anymore, and yours don't have to be either. Is this speaking to you right now? Have you been any of the places I've described? God is so inconceivably faithful. He has not done a single thing for me that He is not ready and anxious to do for you. Hear His tender voice speak to you now. "Take courage! It is I. Don't be afraid."

Trust Him with every inch of your past, present, and future! Until you do, you are susceptible to seduction.

Dear friend, is any area in your life still a weakness? Perhaps you have already confessed it and asked God to forgive you, but you have never asked God to heal you completely, redeem your past, restore your life, sanctify you entirely and

Repented sin can no longer be used against us, but they may still be weaknesses.

help you to forgive your past. Would you be willing to do that now? If so, write a prayer below expressing the desire of your heart.

_____

_____

_____

_____

3 BEING AWARE OF SATAN'S SCHEMES

Put on the full armor of God so that you can take your stand against the devil's schemes. —Ephesians 6:11

Why in the world would God allow someone with wholehearted and sincere and pure devotion to Christ to get caught in the snare of demonic seduction? Even the less mature believer can make sense of the fact that God develops strength in His children through various trials and tribulations, but demonic seduction? What purpose could it possibly serve? After all, it doesn't even seem fair, does it?

You see, we're not talking about your usual brand of temptation when we're addressing the seduction of the saints. Daily we have all sorts of challenges and temptations, some a little more intense than others, but under average conditions many godly people walk steadfastly for the duration without much of a hitch. Not in perfection, of course. But in victory.

We're talking about something in this study that many believers have not experienced. Yet, that is. Perhaps they never will. Wouldn't that be nice? It sure would, but I wouldn't put all my eggs in that happy basket. Not considering the generation we are living in. Anyone with a hint of spiritual discernment can feel the heat rising. I think we'd better do everything we can to fortify ourselves in case we get targeted.

Everyday temptation and intentional demonic seduction are as different as a snowball and an avalanche.

The difference between our everyday temptations and a pointed, intentionally destructive demonic seduction is the difference between a snowball and an avalanche. We can see the added intensification in varying seasons of attack even in the earthly life of Christ. He no doubt had temptations on an ongoing basis but perhaps nothing compared to the full-scale season of temptation in the wilderness.

In the following example, circle clues that suggest this man was being seduced.

I heard a testimony recently about a dear pastor in his early 60s who had walked with God uprightly all his believing life. Although he had amazing compassion for a man who had never really experienced failure, he had no reference point for understanding how Christian people could get into some of the messes he had counseled. He was a very godly man and was neither boastful of his good track record nor judgmental of others who were slightly muddier. In the inmost places of his heart and mind, he simply did not understand.

When this pastor reached his late 50s, something totally unexpected happened. A season of darkness fell upon him: an indescribable heaviness of spirit that neither he nor others could tie to anything circumstantial or physiological. As if the darkness and depression were not enough to cope with, he then began to struggle with lustful, truly pornographic thoughts unlike anything he had ever experienced. Even his teen years had presented him with nothing like the temptations he faced with total astonishment in his late 50s. He was literally bombarded with evil thoughts.

If this man were to come to you for counseling, how would you have counseled him with the information you have been given?

_____

_____

_____

Praise God, he endured the months of suffering and temptation without physically committing adultery, but he did temporarily succumb to uncharacteristic behavior, and those around him were not unaffected. As the season ended, he was personally devastated and found himself asking the question so many others have asked: "What was that?" That, dear sisters in Christ, was seduction. If my hunch is right, things of this nature will only increase in number, which is why we must be warned and fortified.

As we reflect on our previous day's study, what makes this pastor's situation fairly frightening is that I'm unaware of any of the four areas of susceptibility. That's one reason I want to make clear that those who aren't among the high-risk believers are still not immune. No doubt, this man's low-risk profile guarded him against more grievous trespasses in his season of temptation, but it did not keep him from being bombarded.

Thankfully, this precious man of God has experienced the tender mercies of Jehovah Rapha, and he actively serves God, as he should. Our question in this chapter, however, is why would God allow a man of his character to be assaulted by the evil one in the manner that he was?

Although Ephesians 6 does not tell us why, it certainly alerts us to the reality of a dangerous enemy and a furious war. No matter how many times you have read the following Scriptures, I ask you to read them again slowly and reflectively, not giving way to the rubber flesh of familiarity.

Read the following Scripture, underlining the phrases that speak most to you.

"In conclusion, be strong in the Lord [be empowered through your union with Him]; draw your strength from Him [that strength which His boundless might provides]. Put on God's whole armor [the armor of a heavy-armed soldier which God supplies], that you may be able successfully to stand up against [all] the strategies and the deceits of the devil. For we are not wrestling with flesh and blood [contending only with physical opponents], but against the despotisms, against the powers, against [the master spirits who are] the world rulers of

> Even believers who have a low risk for seduction are not immune.

this present darkness, against the spirit forces of wickedness in the heavenly (supernatural) sphere. Therefore put on God's complete armor, that you may be able to resist and stand your ground on the evil day [of danger], and having done all [the crisis demands], to stand [firmly in your place]" (Eph. 6:10-13, AMP).

What admonition does Paul give in these verses?

_____

Why are we to put on the armor of God?

_____

What are we not wrestling with?

_____

List the things we do wrestle with:

_____

_____

Where *The Amplified Bible* uses the words "strategies and the deceits of the devil," the KJV uses the words "wiles of the devil." The NIV and the NASB both employ the word *schemes*. Whether translated "strategies," "wiles," or "schemes," these come from the Greek word *methodeia*. Below are several different definitions offered by various translation experts. Take a moment to meditate on the magnitude of what they are suggesting.

- The word means: "Schemes, wiles, strategies and tricks; trickery. It means the deceits, craftiness, trickery, methods, and strategies which the devil uses to wage war against the believer. Practical Application: The enemy is the devil. … He will do everything he can to deceive and capture the believer."[3]
- "[comp. 'method']; travelling over, i.e. travesty (trickery): -wile, lie in wait."[4]
- "Method, the following or pursuing of an orderly and technical procedure in the handling of a subject."[5]

Which of these definitions concerns you most?

_____

No matter how often I've seen or even shared the definitions of *methodeia*, my skin crawls every time. I hope you absorbed the concept soberly. The most obvious English word found in the Greek is *method*. If we could only understand that the devil does not work haphazardly but carefully, methodically, weaving and spinning, and watching for just the right time. He truly has method to his madness. He draws out plans and executes them very carefully. He carefully sets traps for the express purpose of wreaking destruction in the lives of the saints.

Earlier we discussed that anything God does, Satan attempts to counterfeit. One of the first biblical principles most believers learn concerning their new agenda is that God has a plan for their lives. Please hear this with your whole heart, believer: so does Satan.

Satan watches and waits for just the right time to attack.

Read Jeremiah 29:11 below and then write what you believe Satan's plans for you to be.

God: "I know the plans I have for you," declares the Lord, "plans to prosper you and not to harm you, plans to give you hope and a future" (Jer. 29:11).

Satan: "For I know the plans I have for you," declares the devil,

_____

_____

I described Satan's plans like this: "plans to totally bankrupt you and to harm you, plans to make you hopeless and to destroy your future."

What is the difference between God's plan for our lives and Satan's plan?

_____

_____

Somehow in the life of the dear brother I mentioned earlier, Satan had devised a scheme toward that probable and general goal. To the glory of God, Satan didn't destroy the pastor's future, but he certainly played havoc on that present season. The late 50s may have seemed untimely to the pastor, but it was the perfect time to the enemy. Often our times of assault will come when we're least expecting them. But why does God allow them at all? Since God's ways are so much higher than ours and His thoughts so far beyond us, we won't wholly be able to answer this question. God has ordained that a certain amount of mystery shroud the full understanding of His sovereignty. Put in simple language, we simply do not have the tools to understand God. We can, however, discover some answers that are available to us.

If you have ever been seduced, think back to the way your seduction unfolded. List below the method Satan used to get to you.

_____

_____

Let's be perfectly clear that God never appoints us to sin. Even when He tests His children, His purpose is to prove godly character ... or perhaps to show us the lack thereof. If a test proves a lack, God's chief desire is to enlist the cooperation of the child and provide what is lacking. God never tempts us to sin, nor does He ever fail to provide a way of escape, just as He promised in 1 Corinthians 10:13. Scripture is clear that we are tempted through two sources.

Read 1 Thessalonians 3:5 and James 1:14. What are the two sources of temptation?

_____

_____

45

Needless to say, they work most effectively in tandem, which is why Satan does everything he can to awaken the lusts of his target. In our next lesson, we are going to see scriptural evidence exists that Satan has to gain permission to wage war against a believer in Christ.

As you end today's study, ask God for spiritual discernment so that you will be aware of Satan's schemes.

4 THE TESTING OF JOB

The LORD said to Satan, "Very well, then, everything he has is in your hands, but on the man himself do not lay a finger. —Job 1:12

Both Old and New Testament Scripture support the idea that Satan has to gain God's permission to wage an all-out war upon one of His redeemed. Job 1 is a perfect Old Testament example. Do you know that many scholars believe the Book of Job is one of the oldest books of the Bible? I find that very significant since it concerns a man, His God, and an unseen war.

Read Job 1:1-12 and answer the following questions.

1. How is Job described in verse 1? _____

2. What do you learn about Job from verse 3? _____

3. Who came with the angels to the LORD (v. 6)? _____

4. What did the LORD say to Satan (v. 7)?

_____

5. What was Satan's reply (v. 7)? _____

6. What did the LORD say to Satan in verse 8? _____

7. How did Satan respond in verses 9-11? _____

8. What did the LORD tell Satan in verse 12?_____

9. What did Satan do (v. 12)? _____

For the rest of the story, read Job 1:13-22. Match the messages with either messenger 1, 2, 3, or 4 in the following.

Messenger _____: "The fire of God fell from the sky and burned up the sheep and the servants, and I am the only one who has escaped to tell you!" (v. 16).

Messenger _____: "Your sons and daughters were feasting and drinking wine at the oldest brother's house, when suddenly a mighty wind swept in from the desert and struck the four corners of the house. It collapsed on them and they are dead" (vv. 18-19).

Messenger _____: "The oxen were plowing and the donkeys were grazing nearby, and the Sabeans attacked and carried them off. They put the servants to the sword too!" (v. 14).

Messenger _____: "The Chaldeans formed three raiding parties and swept down on your camels and carried them off. They put the servants to the sword" (v. 17).

What a day! I'm worn out, what about you? The older I get, the more unsettling it seems. Do you realize Job endured the entire excruciating ordeal without ever knowing he was in the middle of a match between the God of the universe and the head dragon of hell? Even at the conclusion of the Old Testament book, Job still had no idea. He had learned plenty about the sovereignty of God, but he still had no concept of the faith God had shown in him. Don't you think Job would have had an easier time if God had said, "Listen, son. I know this is horribly painful, but something much bigger than you know is at stake here. You are a truly righteous man in an unrighteous world. Satan thinks you'll crumble if I draw back some of your protection and blessing. I want him to see that you won't. So, as hard as this is, you stand firm! All the hosts of heaven are rooting for you, and all the unholy hosts of hell are jeering at you. Win a big one for the team, won't you?"

How would you feel in a time of testing to hear such a speech from God?

_____

_____

_____

That kind of explanation would have made a tremendous difference to me. What could be more motivating than a fierce spirit of competition? Right this minute, I'm picturing a replay of the climactic last scene of the movie *Rudy*. All the main character ever wanted to do was play football for Notre Dame. He gets accepted to the school but isn't good enough for the team. Finally they let him attend practice. Before long the other players see that he has spunk even if he lacks size. It's the last game of his senior year, and he finally gets to suit up. The game is almost over. The teammates are watching the clock, hoping the coach will put him in the game. Suddenly the team and the fans begin cheering, "Rudy! Rudy! Rudy!" It's the last play of the game. The coach sends him out on the field, and the little runt in a big Notre Dame football uniform runs with every ounce of energy he has across the field while his daddy cheers in the stands.

Keith and I bawl every time we watch that movie, sitting transfixed until the credits roll. Our favorite part is when the words on the screen say that no one else has ever been carried off the football field by a Notre Dame team. Just Rudy. If I keep thinking about it, I may have to bawl again. We and countless others have watched that movie over and over. Why? Oh, go ahead—admit it. We all want to be a Rudy! Wouldn't that be the ultimate?

If we knew the stakes were high and we were in the middle of a paramount competition, we would throw everything we had into it, wouldn't we? The fact is, we are in such a competition. We just don't realize it. Neither did Job. I have wondered over and over what his face looked like when he got to heaven and they told him what was going on in the unseen world while he was down below. Surely God still has that scene on videotape because I want to check it out and watch it one heavenly day.

Don't you know that Job was so thankful he had chosen to believe God and remain faithful? Can you imagine how strangely Job must have felt to realize he had been chosen by God to fight one of the most difficult earthly battles in history? In humanly inexplicable ways, God allowed Job to be tested so harshly because He, God, had faith in him, Job. Amazing.

We're not out of our reach doctrinally to assume that the same huge competition in the heavenlies takes place all around us. That's exactly what Ephesians 6:10-12 says. Who's to say when things really get tough that we, and countless other believers, have not momentarily been chosen to prove faithful to God? You and I have no idea what's going on in the unseen world when we're being attacked. If we were in the middle of that kind of competition, wouldn't we want to win? I love knowing God's team is always going to win, but I want to be part of the victory myself. Rudy's team had won lots of games, but plenty of teammates had blown their plays.

When Satan turns up the heat, I often say something like this to myself: You have no idea what's going on out there, old girl. This could be really important. Stand firm and don't give the yell leaders of hell anything to cheer about. God is for you. Back up a second. Do you realize God is for you? Yes, the stakes are high. Yes, the battle is rough and sometimes seems unbearable, but God is always for us. Then why does He let our opponents hit us so hard? To prove that we, though mere mortal flesh and blood and terribly self-centered by nature, really are for God.

Perhaps right about now, you're feeling sick inside thinking, *But I've already blown my play. I failed my test.* Listen here, brother or sister. Do you want to talk about someone who has blown some plays? I have! But I'm thankful to say God didn't take me off the team. He took me to the locker room, gave me a little chewing out, a lot of coaching, a little cheering, and sent me back onto the field. His strategy seemed to be making the competition tougher and tougher until I had to toughen up or die. To the glory of God, I have made most of my plays since then. Sometimes they're awkward, late, and not very pretty, … but the points still count.

What encourages you most about the ideas we've been discussing?

_____

_____

_____

Are you still living? Then there's still time on the clock. Are you still a Christian? (And I would remind you that God doesn't abandon His children [Phil. 1:6].) Then you haven't been taken off the team. Get up and fight! God wants to prove to the kingdom of hell that you will get up and you will prove faithful to God. You must! Those who have been wholeheartedly, sincerely, and purely devoted to Christ, no matter how they've been knocked down, will not stay under that pile of opposing players. They will call upon the power of their God and get up. And the players of hell will go flying. I really like that part. Maybe because I owe them some massive hits.

Believers may momentarily be chosen to prove faithful to God.

Somehow I am helped when I remember that a battle between the kingdom of God and the kingdom of darkness is going on around me and I might momentarily be called on to make a play. The old spirit of competition kicks in, and it brings the Rudy right out in me. I am utterly amazed at the character of Job to remain so faithful when he faced such hardship at the hand of Satan.

Job provides the primary Old Testament story of God's permissive will for Satan to unleash a full-scale attack on the redeemed. What about the New Testament? Ah, now that one's easy. It happened to one of my best friends. We will look at him next.

What about you? Have you been called on to make a play and blown it? If so, confess it to God right now and accept His forgiveness. Now get up and get back into the game … the clock is ticking. Win one for the King!

5 THE SIFTING OF PETER

"Simon, Simon, Satan has asked to sift you as wheat. But I have prayed for you, Simon, that your faith may not fail. And when you have turned back, strengthen your brothers." —Luke 22:31-32

You have to understand, if I'm writing a Bible study, I don't get out much. Sometimes I spend more time back in the world of Scripture than I do out in my own. I have a feeling God thinks I'm safer if I stay inside. He's proved right. Some of these Bible figures have become like good buddies. Peter's one of them. He's given me a lot of hope through the years. He spent a lot of his time with Christ big on passion and small on smarts. Been there.

Of course, Peter did have some huge moments. Read Matthew 16:15. What did Christ ask His disciples?

_____

Peter moved right up to the front of the class with his answer. What did he say in Matthew 16:16?

_____

Now read Matthew 16:17-19, and don't you dare ruin it by reading it like you've read it a thousand times! Really take it in.

What did Jesus say to Peter in these verses? _____

_____

_____

Wow. No matter what our differing doctrinal stands may be, surely that's big by any standard. God builds the church on Jesus Christ (1 Cor. 3:11) and the testimony the disciples would preach concerning Him (Matt. 28:19), but no doubt Christ was going to make Peter a major player.

The next thing you know, Peter's shaking his rebuking finger in the face of Jesus for telling them that He (Christ) had many things to suffer, then He'd be killed. In another startling moment that I hope to see on celestial video, "Jesus turned and said to Peter, 'Get behind me, Satan! You are a stumbling block to me; you do not have in mind the things of God, but the things of men' " (Matt. 16:23).

Fast forward to the time when the things Christ prophesied began to be fulfilled at the Passover meal, and Jesus told them that one among them would betray Him. They began questioning who would ever do such a thing, then the discussion descended into a dispute about which of them was considered to be greatest.

In the verses below, underline Satan's request and circle Jesus' prayer for Peter.

"Simon, Simon, Satan has asked to sift you as wheat. But I have prayed for you, Simon, that your faith may not fail. And when you have turned back, strengthen your brothers."
   But he replied, "Lord, I am ready to go with you to prison and to death."
   Jesus answered, "I tell you, Peter, before the rooster crows today, you will deny three times that you know me" (Luke 22:31-34).

Read Luke 22:56-62. Within only a few hours, what had Peter done?

_____

Satan has to get permission to launch a full-scale attack on one of God's children.

The implications of this account are huge to anyone who considers him or herself a follower of Jesus Christ. I believe that Satan had to obtain permission to move outside his usual perimeters and launch a full-scale attack on one of God's children. That permission was granted is obvious in Christ's use of the words " *'when you have turned back,* strengthen your brothers' " (emphasis mine).

Thinking back to our previous lesson, what basic facts can we compile from Job's long nightmare and this unparalleled moment in Peter's life?

_____

_____

How could those facts help us deal with temptation?

_____

_____

_____

First, we see that Satan can and does seek permission to launch excessive attacks on the children of God. Second, we see that God can and sometimes does grant Satan permission to launch such attacks.

But wait a minute. I thought Christ was always for us. If He knew Peter was going to blow it, why did He let the opposition come at him like that? Both Job and Peter were wholeheartedly, sincerely, and purely devoted men of God. Agreed? We've never claimed that those who are wholeheartedly, sincerely, and purely devoted to Christ are perfect. No mortal is. Peter may not have had Job's maturity, but he was a sincere follower of Jesus Christ who left family and occupation to follow Christ. You didn't see the other disciples take a few steps on the water, did you? I'd say Peter qualified for wholehearted, sincere, and pure devotion.

Peter's devotion was pure even when some of the rest of his character needed a little work. He was a pretty good guy. Of course, I'm partial. He's a good friend of mine.

All bias aside, what did Job and Peter have in common?

_____

_____

If you answered something like, "they were each tested by God through Satan," then you are right. (Is that a scary thought, or what?) I'd like to suggest that Peter's encounter with the evil one wasn't just a test. Scripture promises we all will be tested.

According to Job 23:10 and 1 Peter 1:7, what is the purpose for our testing?

_____

Do you suppose it was a coincidence that God inspired both Job and Peter to pen the analogy of refining like gold?

_____

Hopefully no other child of God will ever have to endure the totality of Job's testing, but none of us will escape some degree of it. I'm suggesting, however, that Peter's test was of a specific variety: it was a sift. Only one reason exists why God would give Satan permission to sift a dearly loved, devoted disciple: because something needs sifting.

Don't even read further until you have completely absorbed that statement. God's answer to Satan's petition to sift Peter as wheat would have been denied had Peter not contained something that needed sifting.

Peter had an awesome call of Christ on his life. Christ even called him Petros. A chip off the old block. Before the dust could settle and Peter could tell the Mrs. what Christ had said, the same Jesus blurted, " 'Get behind me, Satan!' " (Matt. 16:23).

Had Christ made a mistake in choosing Peter? Was He sorry? Hardly. He'd made no mistake. Christ knew exactly what He was doing. He also knew what each of the disciples was capable of doing.

Here's the awesome part: Christ obligated Himself to making His true followers what He called them to be. Actually, He still does. Christ told Peter that he would be a powerhouse, and He meant it. Christ also knew that Peter had no means whatsoever of becoming the person He had called him to be. Like all of us, Peter was far too weak in his natural self (Rom. 6:19).

Read 1 Thessalonians 5:23-24. What does the last sentence say?

_____

> Believers who are wholeheartedly, sincerely, and purely devoted to Christ are still not perfect.

> God sometimes allows Satan to sift us because we have something that needs sifting.

Christ called Peter knowing every flaw in him. He gave that flawed apostle a new assignment and a new name. By heaven, the call would be accomplished even if Christ had to do it Himself. I believe Jesus loved Peter's passion, but His cherished disciple also had some ingredients that could prove less palatable to the call. Everything standing between Simon the fisherman and Peter the rock needed to go.

Satan had a sieve. Christ had a purpose. The two collided. Satan got used. Peter got sifted. For reasons only our wise, trustworthy God knows, the most effective and long-lasting way He could get the Simon out of Peter was a sifting by Satan. He was right. You see, the One who called us is faithful, and He will do whatever it takes to sanctify us to fulfill our callings. Yes, it's that important. Remember, huge things are going on out there that we just don't understand.

To me, the sifting of Peter can easily and with sound theology be compared to a full-scale attack by Satan on those with wholehearted, sincere, and pure devotion to Christ. Christ loves all of us with everything in Him. No, we're not among those first disciples, but you and I have been called to be disciples or followers of Christ in our own generations. He is just as watchful and protective over us.

I believe God allows Satan a certain amount of leash where believers are concerned, but I am convinced that if he wants more than his daily allowance, he has to get permission. None of us is less important to Christ than Peter, John, or the apostle Paul. He would never take lightly one of Satan's attacks on His followers. For Satan to launch a full-scale attack of seduction on a wholehearted, sincere, and purely devoted follower of Christ, I believe he has to get permission.

So now we return to the original question: Why would God allow someone with a wholehearted, sincere, and pure devotion to Christ to get caught in the snare of demonic seduction? Because, not unlike Peter, something needs removing, sifting, or changing that an intense encounter with the kingdom of hell would best accomplish. I believe this with all my heart, first of all, because it is congruent with Scripture, and second, because I am convinced it happened to me.

Beloved, are you being sifted? Has God permitted the enemy to launch a full-scale attack against you? God knows what He's doing. He isn't looking the other way, and He's not being mean to you. Maybe this is the only way He can get you to attend to the old so He can do something new. Grab onto Him for dear life! Give Him full reign to remove anything in you that needs to go. Hasten the end of the process. Sift, dear one. Sift!

Have you ever experienced a time of sifting? ☐ Yes ☐ No

If so, describe in as much or as little detail as you would like.

_____

_____

_____

_____

_____

Christ loves all of us with everything in Him.

Video Response Sheet
GROUP SESSION 2

1. God is ever after proving us _____.

2. As the latter days approach:

   A. The enemy is _____.

   B. God _____ to get the _____ ready.

3. Some things can only occur in your life through _____.

4. God will never allow the enemy to sift any _____ that does not need something _____.

5. God is after turning us inside out to put truth in our _____ _____.

6. Satan hates anyone who learns to be _____ with the sword of the Spirit.

7. Instead of _____ your monster down, let God _____ with it.

8. God's Word applies to our _____ _____.

WEEK THREE
THE WATCHMAN

DAY 1
Seduce-Proofing Our Lives

DAY 2
Seduce-Proofing, Part 2

DAY 3
Strong Walls

DAY 4
Secret Places

DAY 5
The Safe House of Love

We are living in radical times. We have entered the age of escalation: escalating evil, escalating deception, escalating seduction, and thankfully an escalating outpouring of the Holy Spirit. God has not left us ill-equipped to stand victoriously while surrounded by ever-increasing wickedness. The Word of God gives us the strategy we need to seduce proof our lives. Let's learn how to guard ourselves against the destruction of the enemy.

PRINCIPAL QUESTIONS

Day 1: According to 2 Corinthians 1:18-20, why does Paul say his preaching was clear rather than vacillating?

Day 2: What did Paul pray regarding blamelessness in 1 Thessalonians 5:23?

Day 3: What does Paul warn us not to do in Ephesians 4:30?

Day 4: What does Romans 8:6 say about the mind controlled by the Spirit?

Day 5: In Mark 12:28-32 what did Jesus say is the most important command?

1 SEDUCE-PROOFING OUR LIVES

May God himself, the God of peace, sanctify you through and through. May your whole spirit, soul and body be kept blameless at the coming of our Lord Jesus Christ. The one who calls you is faithful and he will do it.
—1 Thessalonians 5:23-24

This week we will learn to the best of our biblical knowledge how to seduce-proof our lives. First Thessalonians 5:23-24 holds the key that locks the gate where seduction creeps in.

> Read today's Scripture above. While you're at it, go ahead and write it on an index card and begin to memorize it.

Let's allow God to write this Scripture in permanent marker on our hearts. Then even if our ships get off course and we find ourselves in an ocean of vulnerability, it will serve as a lighthouse to guide us back to safe harbor.

In these verses the terms *spirit, soul,* and *body* encompass every part of our lives. In fact, I am convinced that the very essence of wholeness means our whole spirit, soul, and body sanctified through and through. You may ask, "Where is the reference to the heart and the mind?" In this verse, the soul includes both. Our spirits give us the capacity to know, hear, and have a relationship with God. When differentiated from the spirit, the soul encompasses everything else immaterial about us.

What do you think it means to be sanctified through and through?

_____

We're going to widen our scope on this powerful chapter by looking at the verses in 1 Thessalonians 5:16-25. Here we find one of the most concentrated segments of Scripture in the entire New Testament that describes exactly what you and I are looking for: a seduce-proofed believer.

As you read the verses below, circle words or phrases that describe ways to become a seduce-proofed believer.

"Be happy [in your faith] and rejoice and be glad-hearted continually (always); Be unceasing in prayer [praying perseveringly]; Thank [God] in everything [no matter what the circumstances may be, be thankful and give thanks], for this is the will of God for you [who are] in Christ Jesus [the Revealer and Mediator of that will]. Do not quench (suppress or subdue) the [Holy] Spirit; Do not spurn the gifts and utterances of the prophets [do not depreciate prophetic revelations nor despise inspired instruction or exhortation or warning]. But test and prove all things [until you can recognize] what is good; [to that] hold fast. Abstain from evil [shrink from it and keep aloof from it] in whatever form or whatever kind it may be. And may the God of peace Himself sanctify you through and through [separate you from profane things, make you pure and wholly consecrated to God]; and may your spirit and soul and body be preserved sound and complete [and found] blameless at the coming of our Lord Jesus Christ (the Messiah). Faithful is He Who is calling you [to Himself] and utterly trustworthy, and He will also do it [fulfill His call by hallowing and keeping you]. Brethren, pray for us" (1 Thess. 5:16-25, AMP).

A CONCISE PROFILE OF A SEDUCE-PROOFED CHRISTIAN

This powerful Scripture provides a picture of what a seduce-proofed life looks like. Let's consider each element of this description. First note of the seduce-proofed believer:

1. He is happy in his faith.
1 Thessalonians 5:16. "Rejoice always!" (HCSB).

I want to shout hallelujah with you before I even have a chance to explain what we have to shout about! Dear one, when did someone who is fairly balanced in Scripture last tell you that this faith thing isn't only about sacrifices and continually delayed gratification? The apostle Paul seemed to be saying, "For heaven's sake, be happy in your faith! That's one reason you have it!"

Let's take this opportunity to expose another good example of a doctrine of demons. Too many of us somehow believe that we lack maturity if we wish that the Christian life weren't just good for us like a bowl of bran but that it could also occasionally make us happy like a chocolate malt!

That voice in your ear has been lying all this time. Guess what? You have complete biblical permission to be happy in your faith and also to do the unthinkable—be bold enough to ask why if you're not!

We have complete biblical permission to be happy in our faith!

Are you happy in your faith? ☐ Yes ☐ No ☐ Not sure

Why or why not?

_____

_____

_____

We're going to discover that the characteristic of happiness in the seduce-proofed Christian is tied to another element in the list. Therefore, I'm going to pull it out of scriptural order and give it to you next.

2. She abstains from evil.
1 Thessalonians 5:22. "Stay away from every form of evil" (HCSB).

God gives us the power to abstain from evil by being happy in our faith. Certainly many other things can add happiness to our lives, but they are detoxified and made safe to believers when their primary source of happiness is faith in Jesus. Without happiness in Christ, any other source of joy can become a tool for seduction. Nothing will make you consistently happier than a vibrant relationship with Jesus Christ.

God gives us the power to abstain from evil by being happy in our faith.

Read 2 Corinthians 1:18-20. Why does Paul say his preaching was clear rather than vacillating?

_____

_____

The reason we are so pulled to the no's is because we have never filled our lives with the Yes! Sure, there are no's such as abstain from evil, but we won't be nearly as tempted when we're happy in our faith, rejoicing and glad-hearted. We have a yes God who says no only to things that aren't worthy of His children and don't fit into their own personal 1 Corinthians 2:9s.

Read 1 Corinthians 2:9. Now take your pen and write your name by it.

That's exactly what God wants your reality to be. After your side trip, notice what else is characteristic of the protected Christian:

3. He is unceasing in prayer.
1 Thessalonians 5:17. "Pray without ceasing."

By "pray without ceasing" Paul really didn't have in mind repetitive, wearying formulas. He was talking about a perpetual line of open communication with God throughout the entire day. We're not given to this kind of mentality naturally, so I'm convinced that we have to learn how to pray unceasingly. Mind you, this one will be an ongoing pursuit and one we aren't likely to master, but isn't prayer just that? A pursuit?

A pray-without-ceasing relationship means seeing everything against the backdrop of God's presence.
- A rain shower reminds us of God.
- A difficulty at work makes us turn our thoughts to Him.

A pray-without-ceasing relationship with God keeps communication lines open.

- The first bite of pecan pie makes us thank the God who gave us the gift of taste.
- A near-empty gas tank keeps us hanging tight with God as we coast on fumes to the station.

Everything and anything. Even listening to a powerful worship CD while you're putting dishes in the dishwasher can be prayer without ceasing. Constant communication. Sometimes saying a lot, sometimes saying a little, but living every moment of life as if He were right there. After all, He is, isn't He?

What does the concept of praying unceasingly mean to you?
☐ Bores me to tears   ☐ Excites me
☐ Makes me nervous   ☐ I wonder if I can do it.
☐ Only for the spiritually mature   ☐ I want to begin now!

So what does unceasing communication have to do with protecting ourselves from the enemy? Ah, how often do loneliness and insecurity open a soul to seduction? Our next exhortation, however, actually helps greatly to combat loneliness and insecurity.

4. She is thankful and gives thanks.
1 Thessalonians 5:18. "Give thanks in everything" (HCSB).
Seduce-proofed people live in active gratitude. When we've turned the last page of this study, I pray that every one of us will know by heart that dissatisfaction is a stronghold waiting to happen. An unsatisfied soul should never be ignored. Ongoing or chronic feelings of dissatisfaction are waving red flags that need to be well inspected. Such feelings may mean something vital is missing, and we need to seek God without delay.

Other times, nagging dissatisfaction can be little more than the by-product of living in an overindulged society. Think about it. Advertisers spend countless millions of dollars annually to convince people that we are not yet satisfied. Since our hearts are deceptive in their natural form, sometimes our feelings tell us we're less satisfied than we really are.

Many times we don't have a knowledge problem; we have an obedience problem. Be thankful and give thanks. Do you hear what Paul is saying? Just trying to sit like a thankful-looking bump on a dead log won't cut it. Actively give thanks.

Pause now and make a list of things for which you are thankful.

_____

_____

_____

_____

5. He doesn't quench the Spirit.
1 Thessalonians 5:19. "Don't stifle the Spirit" (HCSB).
Nothing will be more important to us in seduce-proofing our lives than practicing the Holy Spirit-filled or controlled life. We are absolutely incapable of consistent victory on our own. Half-filled is still half-empty. Without the full empowerment of the Holy Spirit, we have no defense against the enemy's schemes.

Sometimes we feel we are less satisfied than we really are.

The only spirit that can overcome seducing spirits is the Holy Spirit. When we quench Him, we're standing in front of Goliath with God whispering into our hard little heads, "I think you might need to know that you're basically on your own here. If you need any help, let Me know."

I can't resist sharing the NIV translation: "Do not put out the Spirit's fire." Whether we realize it or not, God formed each of us with a wick just waiting to be lit. He created us for the fire of the Holy Spirit! If we quench His fire, we'll look for another one elsewhere. That's when we're liable to get burned. I'm certainly not implying sensual passions alone. Anger, rage, and all manner of lusts are also counterfeit passions or self-built fire starters.

Think back for a moment to a scene captured in Exodus 3. I love that Moses heard the voice of God coming from a burning bush. The fire itself was not what made Moses want to take a second look. A fire wasn't unusual.

Read Exodus 3:3. What sparked Moses' attention to the fire?

_____

The fire was unusual because the flames were not burning up the bush. Hebrews 12:29 says that our God is "a consuming fire." You see, God's is the only fire that can consume an object without eventually destroying it. Anger destroys. Rage destroys. Lust destroys. God's fire isn't destructive. He doesn't feed off of us. He is the I Am, the self-existent One. He invites us to feed off of Him. No other fiery passion in our souls will ever guard us from getting burned.

Looking back over the list from today, in which areas are you weak?

☐ 1   ☐ 2   ☐ 3   ☐ 4   ☐ 5

As you end today's study, ask God to strengthen you in those areas. Thank God that His consuming fire doesn't destroy us, but rather it purifies us. Write your prayer of thanksgiving below.

_____

_____

_____

_____

_____

_____

Only the Holy Spirit can overcome seducing spirits.

2 SEDUCE-PROOFING, PART 2

Who can discern his errors? Forgive my hidden faults. Keep your servant also from willful sins; may they not rule over me. Then will I be blameless, innocent of great transgression. —Psalm 19:12-13

Today we will continue to discover ways to seduce-proof our lives straight from our Scripture in 1 Thessalonians 5:16-25. Take a moment to read these passages and refresh your memory. Then we will begin where we left off yesterday. Circle the things you need to work on as you go through the list today.

6. She does not despise instruction, exhortation, or warning.
1 Thessalonians 5:20. "Don't despise prophecies" (HCSB).

This point is huge. Not only is the seduce-proofed individual a hearer and doer of the Word, she also does not despise the instructions, exhortations, or warnings of those sent by God.

Be alert to godly sources that God may purposely place in your hands.

Keep in mind that these instructions, exhortations, or warnings may not come face-to-face. They may come from a sermon, a Christian radio broadcast, or a Christian book that God has purposely placed in our hands. They may also come from a source less agreeable to our palates.

Don't you just hate when someone you don't even particularly like is right? Not only do I like to pick out the advice I want; I like to pick out who gives it to me! God doesn't always send our favorite messengers with His well-pointed exhortations. We have to learn to listen anyway. We need to be desperate for good advisers, and we also need to be desperate for the humility to receive instruction.

Sometimes we may receive a warning or an exhortation from a godly source that leads us to forego what seemed like a wonderful opportunity. Later we may find ourselves troubled by resentful feelings, wondering if we should have gone against the counsel. Of course, we are always wise to pray diligently through these kinds of conflicts to make absolutely sure any human counsel lines up with God's counsel. If we believe it lines up—even when we don't want it to—we must rest in it and try to avoid second-guessing. We may have no idea until heaven the calamity we avoided.

Seek godly counsel. If the counsel of the wise seems to match the sense you get from the Holy Spirit after much prayer, go with their advice no matter how badly your flesh wants to do otherwise!

Describe a time when you received instruction, exhortation, or warning and you heeded the warning. What was the result?

_____

_____

_____

_____

Describe a time that you failed to heed warning. In retrospect, what should you have done differently?

_____

_____

7. He tests and proves all things until he recognizes what is good.
1 Thessalonians 5:21. "Test all things. Hold on to what is good" (HCSB).

This characteristic is the perfect follow-up to our previous one. If we'll learn to test and prove all things, we'll also come to agreement with God-sent exhortation or warning. I can't think of many characteristics more vital in the profile of the seduce-proofed person.

If we're going to start practicing well-fortified lives, we might need to recognize that the muscle this point represents tends to be weak in most of us. We need to ask God to strengthen it. Keep in mind that He'll probably fortify it the most natural way muscles are strengthened: through exercise and repetition.

God may fortify us through exercise and repetition.

Now I know that good and evil do not always appear black-and-white in our technicolor world. Furthermore, a huge chasm can separate goodwill from God's will. I'm slowly learning to test and prove all things until I can recognize what is good. I still find the wait excruciating at times.

What is the biggest struggle for you in testing things?

_____

So far, we've been drawing a profile of a seduce-proofed believer. Now we've arrived at the very issue that sets this Christian apart and protects him or her from innumerable schemes. All of the other characteristics in the profile are manifestations that this believer does one vital thing:

8. She allows God Himself to sanctify her through and through.
1 Thessalonians 5:23. "May God himself, the God of peace,
sanctify you through and through."

There you have it. Through and through. Our safety, joy, fulfillment, and wholeness are all found in allowing God to completely invade our through and through. Nothing withheld. Nothing off-limits. No part of our lives from birth to death. No part of our beings from conscious to subconscious. No part of our minds. No part of our emotions. Through and through.

Allow God to completely invade your through and through.

I don't mean perfected. I just mean surrendered and under the safekeeping of God's dominion. Sanctification basically means set apart. Anything of our experiences, issues, or weaknesses that we don't deliberately set apart to the safekeeping of Christ's dominion sits like a wide-open target under the nose of the lion.

Can you think of any area of your life that you are withholding from God? Be honest with yourself, God already knows.

_____

_____

Next, note the ninth characteristic I desire for my life.

9. His whole spirit, soul, and body are kept blameless.
1 Thessalonians 5:23. "May your spirit, soul, and body be kept sound
and blameless" (HCSB).

Perfection in this lifetime is not going to happen. Anyway, I don't think Christ's perfection was His primary guard against seduction. His primary guard was that He was totally fulfilled by His Father's love, presence, and will. Developing perfection is not a reasonable or expected earthly hope for mortals, but I'll tell you what can be the goal: blamelessness!

What did Paul pray regarding blamelessness in 1 Thessalonians 5:23?

_____

_____

_____

He whose walk is blameless
is kept safe,
but he whose ways are
perverse will suddenly fall.
—Proverbs 28:18

The psalmists speak often of the coveted condition they describe as "blameless." Read Proverbs 28:18 in the margin. What does it tell us about being blameless?

"He whose walk is blameless is kept _____."

Bingo! That's exactly what we are looking for. How can we be kept safe from seduction? By developing a blameless walk. I know you tire of hearing one impossible dream after another from churchy people, but this one really is attainable. God revealed a Scripture to me that defines a very livable blamelessness. We've already seen its context in a previous lesson. Read Psalm 19:12-13 again.

What is David's inspired definition of blamelessness?
☐ When we are perfect   ☐ When we are sinless
☐ When we see Jesus   ☐ When no willful sin is ruling over us

Living out from under the dominion of willful sin is not only possible; it is our God-given right, our Holy Spirit-empowered reality, and the absolute will of our Father in heaven.

Yes, indeed. He whose walk is blameless is kept safe. So how do we start becoming blameless? By allowing God Himself to sanctify us through and through—our relationships, entertainment, hobbies, and everything else! Our safety is inviting Christ's involvement in everything. He's no bore either. He can get great joy from watching you play tennis. He wants no part of our lives to say, "Keep out!" If He's there, Satan can't touch it.

Let's look at the last two characteristics in our profile of the seduce-proofed person.

10. She knows that the One who called her is faithful and He will do it.
1 Thessalonians 5:24. "He who calls you is faithful, who also will do it" (HCSB).

The seduce-proofed woman has no confidence in her flesh. Nor does she dream that either checking off a list of characteristics or performing a catalog of spiritual disciplines has any power to protect her. She knows that God is faithful, and He will do it.

The seduce-proofed believer simply realizes that obedience places her in the posture God delights to bless. Obedience invites Christ to show His incomparable strength in our mortal weakness.

God delights to bless
our obedience.

Pause and thank God that He is faithful. God will accomplish His will in your life if you will allow Him.

11. He knows he needs prayer.

1 Thessalonians 5:25. "Brothers, pray for us also" (HCSB).

Brothers and sisters, we need prayer. That's all there is to it. Especially as the Day is drawing near!

How many people actively intercede for you on a consistent basis? Write their names below:

_____

_____

If you can't name at least several, get busy enlisting some! Commit to reciprocate, and become an effective intercessor for others. We need one another's prayers desperately. Don't assume that since you've done OK so far without prayer partners that you're not at risk. These are ever-increasing days of wickedness! Start looking.

Commanding us to pray for one another is one of the ways God enforces unity in the body of Christ. Let's make the most of our intercessors. Tell them specific requests. Humble yourself before them and ask them to pray for strengthening weak spiritual muscles. Consider equipping them with Scriptures that you want them to pray until they become realities in your life. Unequaled power can be released when we pray Scripture for one another.

As we conclude today's lesson, could we practice what Paul just preached to us by example? I want you to know that I am praying for every person God will cause to take this study. He knows your name, your motivation for doing the study, and the work He wants to accomplish in you, even if you're studying to help someone else.

May I ask you to do two things that God is placing on my heart? First, please pray right now for someone who once had wholehearted, sincere, and pure devotion to Christ but who is presently caught in a web of seduction. He or she is in such urgent need. Along with any other intercession the Holy Spirit gives you, please pray Ephesians 1:18-19 for this brother or sister.

Also pray, according to Ephesians 5:8-15, that this "sleeper" would "wake up" and that God would mercifully expose the deeds of darkness and expose the precious life to the light so healing can begin.

Write your prayer below:

_____

_____

_____

_____

Finally, would you pray one time for me? Please pray that I will continue to throw myself before God's throne, forsaking all other gods and the approval of men, that my life will be seduce-proofed, that I will not lead people in error, and that I would love His Son more than anything in all of life.

Thank you, Dear One.

> Unequaled power can be released when we pray Scripture for one another.

3 STRONG WALLS

No temptation has seized you except what is common to man. And God is faithful; he will not let you be tempted beyond what you can bear. But when you are tempted, he will also provide a way out so that you can stand up under it. —1 Corinthians 10:13

All this stuff about seduction is really important, but I don't mind telling you, I've got another problem that needs some attention. Keith and I need a new fence. That's all there is to it. Why can't things just stay fixed? We replaced the fence not long after we moved into the house. OK, so it's been nearly 20 years, but it seems like yesterday.

A huge part of our fence problem is coming from the neighbor directly behind us. They innocently planted a small line of trees right against the fence many years ago. Now those trees are about twelve feet tall. Inch by inch, the roots have grown under our fence and into our yard until the uneven ground has completely unearthed the fence posts. The branches that years ago were only twigs have now strengthened until they have dislodged the sturdy nails and pushed the slats right off the horizontal posts. They grew so gradually, we didn't notice until the slats were falling, one right after the other.

Our predicament certainly could be worse. Keith pitched me a magazine the other day and pointed to an article he said I must read. As I did, my eyes grew big as saucers. Another person's fence fell down too. What complicated her situation somewhat is that her property was next to a small wildlife park. Both neighbors had quite a lot of acreage, and she raised miniature horses while her neighbor boasted a variety of exotic animals.

How did she realize part of her fence was down? One day she looked up and a male lion was tearing her favorite horse to shreds for lunch. True story.

We often don't realize our fence is down until Satan devours something precious.

Tragically, we often don't realize part of our fence is down until Satan, the roaring lion, is devouring something precious to us right on our own property. Mind you, he has no right to be on our property, but all he needs for a written invitation is a weak spot in the fence.

What happened to our fence is exactly what happens in many of our lives when the enemy gains ground that does not belong to him. At some point prior to his complete intrusion into our lives, he laid groundwork. Like our neighbors' trees, this groundwork is often so subtle and seems so harmless that we give it very little notice. Inch by inch, the enemy grows something powerful right on the edge of our fence.

Examine your own life. Can you see where the enemy is laying groundwork to defeat you? Maybe it is a relationship, a business deal, an addiction, or something that consumes you. Do you see any areas that need immediate attention? If so, what are they?

_____

_____

_____

We begin to see a few little hints of weakness in the boundary here and there, but with our busy lives we often pay little attention. Here's the big one: we reason that, after all, nothing disastrous has happened before. Listen carefully, never assume that just because a smaller problem hasn't exploded into a bigger problem before, it never will. Wrong.

That's exactly what the enemy wants us to think. Don't ever forget what a schemer he is. He loves nothing better than supplying a false sense of security. One day when we least expect it, we look up and the lion is in the yard and our "pet" is being torn to shreds. Oh, I pray that God will expose every bit of false security we have!

I want to share a visual with you that God gave me based on the Old Testament temple. It has been a great help to me; I pray that it will be to you too. My hope is that we may simplify something that can be complex into more manageable terms. Take a look:

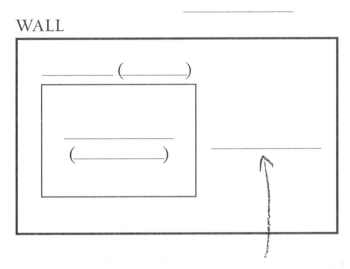

WALL

Above the inside rectangle, place the word *temple*. To me the temple is a perfect illustration for a believer's life because the Word of God tells us that since the cross and Pentecost, the Spirit of God dwells in believers.

The temple perfectly illustrates believers' lives.

According to 1 Corinthians 6:19, what is the temple of God?

_____

_____

Write *my body* in parenthesis beside the word *temple*.

Notice on your diagram the line drawn inside the temple structure. Write the word *possession* on that line. We believers in Christ are represented by the temple structure itself. In fact, the verse just told us that our actual bodies are the temples of the Holy Spirit. Write *the Holy Spirit* under the word *possession*. When we received Christ as our Savior, the Holy Spirit took up immediate residence in us.

What does Romans 8:9 say must be true if you belong to Christ?

_____

_____

Whether or not you realized what was taking place spiritually, when you deliberately received Christ Jesus as your personal Savior, the Holy Spirit of God immediately came to dwell within you. Once God deposits the Spirit of Christ into our bodies, I believe Scripture teaches that we are sealed until we see Christ face-to-face and our redemption is completed in heaven. I believe with all my heart that the Holy Spirit doesn't depart from a believer and that no other spirit can enter us.

According to Ephesians 1:13, how were we marked in Christ?

_____

God's seal is not only a mark of ownership or a stamp with His name on it. I believe it is both of those things and more. Paul drew his terminology from the society of his day. Any document of the king or under his authority was marked with a seal. When the king authorized a document or enclosure, his royal insignia was stamped in the warm liquid of wax or precious metal, and it would quickly harden into a seal. The seal could be opened only by the one to whom it was sent or under the direct authority of the king.

God, the King of heaven and earth, has secured us so that He can present us as a bride for His Son. Nothing and no one on earth or in the heavenlies has the authority or power to break His seal. We are saved for Christ alone. On the day of our complete and perfect redemption, face-to-face with Jesus, we will be safe in the hands of the One to whom we've been sent. Until then, nothing gets in and nothing gets out. Why we sense the Holy Spirit's activity differently at times and may even feel that He is no longer in residence is implied further in the same letter.

Do not grieve the Holy Spirit of God [do not offend or vex or sadden Him], by Whom you were sealed (marked, branded as God's own, secured) for the day of redemption (of final deliverance through Christ from evil and the consequences of sin).
—Ephesians 4:30, AMP

Read Ephesians 4:30 in the margin. What does Paul warn us not to do?

_____

How do you think we can grieve the Holy Spirit?

_____

We quench or grieve the Holy Spirit by refusing His authority over us—by choosing not to yield to Him. He therefore retreats His activity and fullness in us, sometimes even to the point that we may not sense His presence. Still, I believe He neither departs from us nor lies dormant. If the Spirit of Christ is in us, we can't just continue in sin. The absence of both His activity and the feeling of His presence will eventually create such a void— or such havoc—that we will no longer be able to bear it.

Now let's study the other components in the diagram. You can also see ground around the temple structure and a wall.

On the outside of the wall write the word *opposition*.

_____

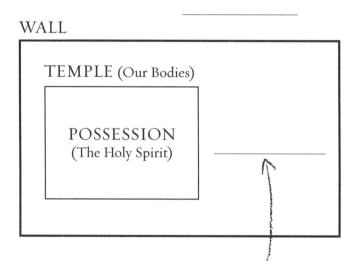

WALL

TEMPLE (Our Bodies)

POSSESSION
(The Holy Spirit)

Opposition is a normal part of our existence while we occupy these mortal bodies. The most victorious, Spirit-filled believers face challenge continually by all sorts of satanic opposition, whether or not they recognize Satan as the source.

What does Ephesians 6:12 say our battle is against?

_____

When we practice victorious lives and allow the sanctifying work of the Holy Spirit to permeate every part of our lives, as a rule (though God can make any exception He chooses) God limits Satan to the outside of that wall. The evil one can work only through opposition.

Don't downplay how powerful opposition can be, however! Opposition is anything that opposes (1) us, (2) the work God desires to do in us, and (3) the work God desires to do through us. Opposition may not even appear oppositional! It may be something that feeds our fleshly pride but opposes everything about who we are in Christ.

Have you ever struggled with opposition from the enemy? If so, how?

_____

_____

Satan cannot get inside our temples, so the closest he can get is inside the wall. What does the wall or the fence line represent to you and me? God's will and obedient lives form that perimeter. We gave this kind of life a name earlier: blamelessness. We can live in a state of being where we are not sinning willfully and no sin has dominion over us.

How does Satan get inside the wall or fence line? He puts pressure on the outside, hoping to get a reaction or some sort of cooperation from the inside. All he needs is one little piece of the fence or wall to crumble, and the lion's in the yard. I believe Satan ordinarily puts pressure on the wall or fence by raising either temptation or turmoil. One or the other can eventually lead to both.

Let's talk about temptation first: Satan can put pressure on the fence (or wall) by raising temptation right at the fence line. Remember when we talked about the importance of being happy and satisfied in our faith? If we don't take Christ up on the fullness of joy and satisfaction within our walls, we are still subject to longing glances at life outside our walls.

What about turmoil? I can speak personally to this one because the enemy used it so effectively in my life. Certainly he has also weakened my wall through temptation, but one of his most powerful schemes against me came through raising turmoil at my fence line. He knew I was an abuse victim whether or not I had ever faced the fact. He raised all sorts of things at the fence line that quickened emotional reactions in me.

Many of the things he raised at the fence line were nothing but lies, but I was too inexperienced to recognize the deception. Had I allowed God to permeate my life with His sanctifying Holy Spirit and heal me through and through, Satan couldn't have evoked such an inside response from me. I cooperated with the devil because I had not completely cooperated with God.

God tried to teach me in easier ways. Since I didn't learn my badly-needed lessons from His Word and easier methods, He found another tool: the devil himself. Satan did everything he could at that fence line to get a reaction from me on the inside of my temple. Why did God let him? He didn't just let him. He used him. Allowing Satan to call the

I cooperated with the devil because I had not completely cooperated with God.

victim buried within me to the surface became such a teaching tool in the hand of God that I could not ignore it. Nor will I ever forget it.

Can you relate with me? What are some lessons you had to learn the hard way?

_____

_____

_____

In Proverbs 25:28 we read, "Like a city whose walls are broken down is a man who lacks self-control." Self-control is one of the qualities of the fruit of the Spirit. What does self-control have to do with the Spirit? Only self can decide who's in control. When self grants control to the Holy Spirit and we live within the boundaries of God's will for our lives, our wall stands firm and Satan must work from more of a distance. He is limited to opposition rather than outright oppression.

Satan hopes to raise such a powerful opposition at the fence line that we lose self-control. In other words, self rejects the control of the Holy Spirit and we give way to things such as anger, bitterness, rage, lust, greed, ambition, and despair.

Whether Satan targets weakness or sin makes little difference to him if he can cause us to temporarily reject the authority and sanctifying power of the Holy Spirit controlling self. If he can accomplish his goal, just one little area of the wall tumbles down. Sometimes nothing happens right away. Satan often waits to wreak havoc while he establishes a sense of false security. Then the rules change. We look up and the lion is in the yard.

Again, Satan cannot enter the temple, but when self starts rejecting the control of the Holy Spirit, a portion of the wall tumbles down and Satan can move from a position of opposition to oppression. Look at your diagram again, and place the word *oppression* on the line inside the wall.

Have you ever been oppressed by the enemy? If so, how?

_____

_____

_____

Though the range can vary, oppression is the closest Satan or his demons can get to a believer. The closer proximity of enemy attack can make the assault almost overwhelming. Satan's voice, silent only to our earthly senses, can scream so loudly that the oppressed think they can't hear the voice of God.

In the next paragraph underline the things we can do to overcome the enemy.

Satan is most assuredly a "powerful enemy" and a foe too strong for me (Ps. 18:17). But he is under Christ's feet. Relief comes only when we cry out with everything in us for Christ to come and take total control, withholding nothing from Him. Complete submission. In all probability we need to submit some things that we have not noticed or that we have ignored. The full authority of Christ reigning over us and through us is exactly what diffuses the power of the oppressor.

Satan hopes that we lose self-control.

Seduction is a form of oppression, of course, but it's a very sly scheme intended to catch us off guard, pitched with mind-boggling velocity from a direction we did not expect. Seduction means the demonic trickery of a professional liar. If you'll allow me to put it this way, seduction is Satan at his best. He's looking for the trickiest means of getting inside our walls, and I doubt he considers anything a greater accomplishment than the broken wall of a devout believer.

Seduction is Satan at his best.

God is a big believer in walls. I believe the need for boundaries or walls came with the entrance of the serpent onto the property of God's children. God the Father threw a wall or boundary around the garden of Eden by the flaming sword of an angel. Later, He instructed the Israelites to build a portable wall around the Old Testament tabernacle. Likewise, the temple had a wall around it, as did the city of Jerusalem. Not coincidentally, even the heavenly Jerusalem described in Revelation 21 has a wall around it (Rev. 21:12-21).

Who does Revelation 21:27 say will enter the heavenly Jerusalem?

_____

_____

God reserves the right to say what gets to enter the gates and what does not. When we establish sturdy walls, we don't have to live in fear. We just let the walls do their jobs. Don't ever forget that Satan can't get in from the outside without an invitation from the inside. Next we'll consider a powerful way he gains access.

Satan can't get in from the outside without an invitation from the inside.

What two lessons that you learned today can you apply to your life next week?

_____

_____

 # SECRET PLACES

Finally, brothers, whatever is true, whatever is noble, whatever is right, whatever is pure, whatever is lovely, whatever is admirable—if anything is excellent or praiseworthy—think about such things. —Philippians 4:8

Returning again to the diagram from our previous lesson, I want you to see with me another parallel drawn from Old Testament Scripture that I find nothing less than startling.

Read Ezekiel 8:1-10,12 and meditate on every word. What did Ezekiel see through the hole in the wall?

_____

_____

Ezekiel 8:7 tells us the Spirit took him to the entrance to the court. The following parallel is not a perfect fit in our temple illustration, but I believe it is worthy of our consideration. I checked in several commentaries in which all the commentators agree that this court is most likely referring to the inner court of the temple. In the parallel you and I are drawing, the temple structure is our self, and the Holy Place might be considered the actual Spirit of God dwelling within us.

I'd like to suggest that the inner court could represent what is private to us without necessarily being sacred. In other words, the secret places. The most secret chamber of our personal lives that we might consider outside the sacred could be the mind. Many of us may not be committing grievous sins with our bodies, but we are entertaining them in the recesses of our minds.

When David the psalmist spoke about the inner parts (Ps. 51:6), he referred to the secret places of the mind and heart (or emotions). After his headlong dive into a pit of sin, he realized how much he needed "truth in the inner parts" and "wisdom in the inmost places." We kid ourselves into thinking that sin is safe in the secret places.

For the believer, I am convinced the mind is often the last inner chamber we allow God to sanctify. One reason is because it is a never-ending challenge to keep clean, and we sometimes adopt the attitude, "Why bother?" Oh, Beloved, we must bother because the mind is the biggest battlefield we have on which our spiritual battles are fought. Even our feelings eventually bow down to our thoughts.

People continually say, "I can't change the way I feel." But, Beloved, if we change the way we think, before long our thoughts change the way we feel. All sin begins in the mind, and untold secret sin is allowed to flourish there. But not without effect. Sooner or later.

Do you think it is possible to have a clean mind? ☐ Yes ☐ No ☐ Not sure

We hear statistics concerning how many impure or negative thoughts go through the typical mind in a 60-second period, and we buy that standard as an immutable truth. The redeemed of God who are inhabited by the very Spirit of Jesus Christ weren't bought by His blood to be typical. No, we can't be perfect or sinless, nor can we find some legalistic means of controlling every thought we have. But can God clean up our negative or impure minds? Yes! Furthermore, if we don't let Him, our minds will taint our hearts and ultimately affect our actions. Remember how the apostle Paul said the serpent could get to those with wholehearted, sincere, and pure devotion to Christ? By seducing and corrupting their minds (2 Cor. 11:2-3)!

We have studied how to fortify ourselves against seduction, but much of our work will be in vain if we don't let God sanctify us through and through—all the way to the inner court of our minds. What are we doing behind the hole in the wall? In the secret places of the mind? In the darkness? What are our idols right there in the inner chambers? Those perhaps no one else knows about? Dear one, is there a mess behind that hole in the wall?

Would you practically die if suddenly your thoughts were somehow exposed to the public?

_____

We've all been there, but we don't all have to stay there. Having our minds sanctified is an ongoing, lifelong process, but absolutely nothing will have a greater harvest in your life. So many people try to get a grip on their emotions, but they don't realize the emo-

The inner court may be private without being sacred.

tions are usually regulated by the mind. If we don't start thinking differently, we will never feel differently.

God loves you with an unfailing love. You cannot diminish His love with impure or negative thoughts, but you can diminish your awareness and enjoyment of His love. Trust Him to go behind that hole in the wall, or you'll never be free!

In Mark 12:28,30, when Christ answered the question, " 'Of all the commandments, which is the most important?' " He answered, " 'Love the Lord your God with all your heart and with all your soul and with all your *mind* and with all your strength' " (emphasis mine).

What do you think loving God with all your mind means?

_____

_____

> You cannot diminish God's love—only your awareness and enjoyment of it.

Love springs from trust. Therefore, loving God with all my mind begins with trusting God with all my mind. It means asking God to come into secret places where I may harbor or practice sin. It means trusting that He's not going to reject me or forsake me or be totally disgusted with me. He already knows, and He wants in. He will not clean it out with a big yard blower from the outside. He cleans up the mind from the inside only.

But, we have to cooperate. How do we do that? We apply the principle of feeding what we want to live and starving what we want to die. In other words, we start feeding the Spirit in us and starving the flesh.

In many discussions I've had with other believers, many still claim what I used to claim: "But I don't feed the flesh." Meanwhile, they (like I used to do) still watch some inappropriate programming, occasional R-rated movies (but "not the really bad kind"), and engage in impure or unedifying conversation and humor.

What are some ways that you feed the flesh?

_____

How could you feed the Spirit and starve the flesh?

_____

_____

Much too often we have adopted a relative standard based on the wickedness of the world rather than the holiness of God. Because we don't do and watch most of the stuff out there, we think our minds are clean. Yet in reality, they are not. One of the seductive lies of Satan is to name things harmless that are anything but.

Here's the deal. We don't know how harmful and effective all these "lesser evils than the really depraved world" are until we've given them up for a while. We think our minds are clean until they really are clean. Can we keep them spotless? No. Clean? Yes!

Please hear me out. We live in radical times. We have waltzed into a season on the kingdom calendar that is unprecedented. We have entered the age of escalation: escalating evil, deception, seduction, and, thankfully, an escalating outpouring of the Holy Spirit. God has not left us ill-equipped to stand victoriously while surrounded by ever-increasing wickedness.

God is arming His people.

We live in a time of unparalleled release of the Word of God on laypeople. Never before has the entire globe experienced such a wave of scriptural equipping. Laypeople all over the world are testifying to a growing hunger for the Word of God. What is God doing? He is arming His people with the sword of the Spirit because we've entered an unprecedented war!

Not coincidentally, God has also equipped us with more uncompromising media and materials than any generation before us have ever had, suited for everything from Christian growth to Christian entertainment. God has not left us ill-equipped, but we have to take Him up on the equipment!

At first the transition is difficult. We have been so overstimulated in the world that we've become desensitized to anything less than "much." When we first make the choice to really allow God to sanctify our minds and we start feeding our spirits rather than our flesh, we can feel the sacrifice. If we'll keep it up, however, soon we'll start reaping some of the benefit.

What does Romans 8:6 say about the mind controlled by the Spirit?

_____

As we begin to get a taste of this effervescent life and genuine mental peace, we have just the motivation we need to keep up the good work. Then our feelings start changing and improving. We often feel better all over. We start feeling full and satisfied. After a while, it's the only life for us, and we don't ever want to go back.

Yes, the kind of transition I'm describing is radical, but we're living in radical times. The lion wants in the yard, and we'd better have a plan to keep him out. Peter learned the hard way how much access the devil wants to devour believers.

What was Peter's advice in 1 Peter 1:13-14?

_____

If you haven't already surrendered to the pursuit of loving God with your whole mind and trusting Him to sanctify your thoughts, why not start now? You will be freer and more contented than you've ever been in your life!

Then through the empowering of His Holy Spirit, start furnishing your mind with "whatever is true, whatever is noble, whatever is right, whatever is pure, whatever is lovely, whatever is admirable … anything [that] is excellent or praiseworthy" (Phil. 4:8). You might be surprised to discover how many things can fall into those categories such as a great play, a night at the symphony, a good book, or a fabulous basketball game. God wants to be in our leisure time as much as He is in our church and our work.

Beloved, sometimes nothing is more spiritual than recreative refreshment! Don't withhold it from Him. Remember, the protective kind of sanctification comes when He is invited into our through and through.

What's out there in the world's entertainment media is only going to get worse. At what point are we going to opt out of its direct influence? We've got a job to do in our dark world. Those people out there are our assignment. How can we minister to them if we're altogether like them? What else but God's lavish presence in our lives will distinguish us from all the other people on the face of the earth (Ex. 33:16)?

What have you got to lose that's not worth the loss?

Fortified lives: from the walls around our courtyards to the secret, inner courts of the mind. What have you got to lose that's not worth the loss? And just wait until you experience the gain!

Outline a plan below to fortify your life. Do you need to deal with weak or secret places? What things do you need to change?

_____

_____

_____

_____

_____

Oh, Beloved. Let's do this thing … and let's do it to the core.

5 THE SAFE HOUSE OF LOVE

"Love the Lord your God with all your heart and with all your soul and with all your mind and with all your strength." —Mark 12:30

I got a bit of a late start writing today. Toward the end of the praise and worship service I attended in the den of my cabin this morning (by myself), I heard the voice of God speak to my heart: "Come and play." I love that He said, "Come" and not, "Go." "Come." That meant He was already there.

I also love how I could tell by the sweet tone of the silent voice whispering to my spirit that He was smiling. You know, you can tell that kind of thing in the voices of those you really know. I can tell you the exact expression on my husband or children's faces when I talk to them on the phone just by the pitch of their voices. It was that way this morning. I could have outlined His expression with my finger.

I don't always hear Him like that. Oh, I wish I did, but I don't. Sometimes we have to walk away from the deafening demands of our chaotic lives to inhale His sweet spirit.

I am so in love with Him. Let me say that again, I am so in love with Him! We look with pained desperation for things that are already there. Dear Seeker, the breeze is already there. The sunset is already there. The morning tide is already there. The timid doe is already there. The summer rain is already there.

Take God's creations personally. They are here for us.

Have you taken them personally? ☐ Yes ☐ Frequently ☐ Seldom ☐ No

_____

Could I make a suggestion? Before going any further in today's lesson, why don't you stop for a few moments and go outside. Listen to the sounds God created just for you, the birds chirping, the wind blowing, the rain falling, the leaves crunching under your feet. Notice the colors in the sky, feel the warmth of the sun or the cold and the crisp air against your face. Give thanks to your Creator who created this day. Worship Him.

Did you do it? Don't say "I'll get to it later." Chances are you won't. Describe your worship experience.

_____

_____

_____

I lived much of my life having no idea how a mortal heart with eyes blinded to the object of their greatest pleasure could be so slain by immortal romance. I will not rest. Hear me. I will not rest until I have told everyone who will listen of this wondrous love. God's love is greater than any earthly love—His true love makes all others seem like shadows. I am jealous with a godly jealousy for every son and daughter of the living God to know and experience this love.

Oh, please listen. I could go to the furthest reaches of human vocabulary and study the languages of every people to find who says it best, and still all my efforts would be frustrated by this divine affection that exceeds description. Yet this love, this lavish love of God, is meant for every mortal creature who has traveled miles on earth to find a carnal affection that simply suffices.

God waits, watches, and hopes that the sun will not set on our days without our standing on tiptoes at the extremity of life, yelling, "Is there not more than this?"

"Ah, yes, my love. There is more."

Oh, Beloved, we sing of this love week after week in our perfectly timed orders of worship while heaven's hosts gather curiously and watch masses of mortals sing in one accord of a love they do not know. Angel faces look upon God, then again upon His children. And their eyes, having no human cataract, behold the actual substance of divine love

> as wet as water,
> but not water,
> as weighty and warm as a woolen cloak,
> yet not woolen,
> and as light and distinct as a snowflake,
> but never cold,
> lavished in heaps upon the very mortals who do not feel it.

A fury rises within me, and my soul shakes its fist. Surely the vilest of all demons' doctrines tells us that love for God, since He is by essence unseen and untouched, is not something you feel. Lies!

What would you tell a new mother who confides in you, "I'm so glad I have her. I waited so long. She is so perfect. So beautiful. I am so grateful she is mine. Truly she has delivered me from my feelings of uselessness and my lack of identity. But I thought I would feel something. I was told I'd feel love. Is it OK that I don't? Is this normal?"

We would tell her to get to her doctor! That something isn't normal. She might be suffering from postpartum depression. Our hearts would break as we see the tears of lack flowing down her face and we realize that her heart is free to feel guilt but strangely shackled from love. We would hold her in our arms while she weeps. We would also weep as we pray pleadings of God over her, then we would assure her of what we know:

This lavish love of God is meant for each of us.

Just because we cannot see or touch God does not mean that we cannot feel love for Him.

74

"Dear, dear mother, your heart was made for love. You just do not yet feel it. Do not despair. It is there. You were not made a mother and not given the love. You are so right to have told me. Now all we must do is discover why you do not feel what is yours to feel."

"You foolish Galatians! Who has bewitched you?" (Gal. 3:1). Who has made us think that all lesser loves which are mere shadows of God's true love can feel while the greater love for which the heart was created is not felt? It simply exists. We sing of it. We speak of it. But we do not feel it.

At the risk of offending thousands of people, I will say again what the Spirit of God bellows in my soul: the bride of Christ suffers from lack of love for her Groom. She admires Him. She respects Him. She is grateful to Him. She's been saved by Him. She is intellectually stimulated by Him. She loves her new clothes. She is enamored by the jewels. But she expected to feel love. Is it OK that she doesn't? Is this normal?

The bride of Christ suffers from lack of love for her Groom.

The bride is suffering from post-deliverance depression. She expected to feel something. Is it OK that she doesn't?

What did Jesus say is the most important command (Mark 12:28-32)?

_____

_____

Masses of believers do not realize that love for God is something they can actually feel. In fact, if we don't, we are frighteningly, staggeringly vulnerable to a counterfeit.

I do not suggest that we feel the constant gush of love for God every waking moment any more than I feel the constant gush of love for my husband and children. Yet, my affection for them is a greater reality than my flesh and bone. There are times, however, when I nearly drown in the gush of divine love and marvel that something so full and so perfect could ever come from something so injured as I.

We experience the first miracle at the wedding of Cana again every time an earthen pitcher full of water pours forth sweet wine. But will we risk letting the wine evaporate in our generation?

As Jesus was sitting on the Mount of Olives, the disciples came to Him privately. " 'Tell us,' they said, 'when will this happen, and what will be the sign of your coming and of the end of the age?' " (Matt. 24:3).

Read Matthew 24:4-8,12-14 to see Jesus' response. What did Jesus say would happen (v. 12)?

_____

_____

One of the most insidious diseases of the latter days will be cold souls. In the Matthew passage, the word *cold* is our translation of the Greek word *psycho.* "It is from this verb that *psyche,* soul, is derived. Hence *psyche* is the breath of a living creature, animal life. *Psycho* occurs only once, in the future passive, meaning to be cool, to grow cool or cold in a spiritual sense, as regards Christian love ([Matt.] 24:12)."[1]

Bride of Christ, we must neither tolerate a lack of love in our souls nor let anyone convince us that it is normal not to feel love for God. The bride was created to love the Groom. Not only is a lack of love for God our heart's most needless tragedy, loving God is our only recourse for divinely loving others.

It is normal to feel love for God.

Love is the stuff of intimacy. We can never learn intimacy in even the most anointed corporate worship. We discover divine love in the inexplicable freedom of solitary confinement with God. We then bring it without so much as a deliberate thought into the great assembly. It simply cannot stay home.

Doctrines of demons will teach you that you can't really find passion in God. They say you cannot really feel spiritual things. They will offer you substitutes, false Christs. " 'Watch out that no one deceives you. For many will come in my name' " (Matt. 24:5). How many have already come to you? What false Christ has failed to fulfill your cavernous soul? Do not be deceived. It is seduction sent to woo you away from the one thing that is real.

**Ask God for love.
Then ask for more.**

Seek the real with everything in you. More than life. More than breath. More than health. More than blessing. More than gifts. Ask for love. Not just once but over and over for the rest of your days. Ask till your voice is hoarse and with shriveled hand you point to your own aged heart and with one dying word whisper, "More."

The only appropriate way to end today's lesson is in prayer. Spend time thanking God for His unfailing love for you. Then ask Him for more. Oh, how He wants to pour out His lavish love on you. Would you let Him?

Write your prayer below:

_____

_____

_____

_____

_____

_____

_____

_____

Video Response Sheet

GROUP SESSION 3

1. We are the _____ of the Holy Spirit.

2. Walls can represent being _____ in or _____ or they can represent

   _____.

3. Some people fall into _____ because of _____.

4. Satan knows that we were _____ to _____ and rebirthed to live

   _____ _____.

5. There is a _____ _____ outside the walls.

6. We become so focused on what we _____ _____ _____ that we miss what

   we _____ _____.

7. There are _____ of _____.

8. The walls around us are the walls of the _____ of God and His _____

   dwells within.

WEEK FOUR
WISE UP!

If we are not careful, out of fear we will become paranoid about developing relationships with others. Believer, beware! That is exactly what the enemy would like for us to do. Jesus came for the express purpose of connecting with people. If we are going to connect, we must learn to develop godly relationships instead of spiritual relationships. As the world grows more depraved, the church must grow more alert, more equipped, more sanctified, and more unified. Join me as we wise up to the enemy's schemes.

PRINCIPAL QUESTIONS

Day 1: What does Paul say about Satan and his servants in 2 Corinthians 11:14-15?
Day 2: In John 17:23, why did Jesus pray for unity among believers?
Day 3: In what ways was the man in Proverbs 7 seduced?
Day 4: What did Jesus warn us about in Matthew 24:4-5?
Day 5: According to Philippians 2:15-16, what is our goal as believers?

1 WARM HEART, WISE HEADS

"As you sent me into the world, I have sent them into the world." —John 17:18

Our focus this week will be guarding against relational seductions and perhaps a host of other kinds of unhealthy relationships by making sure we are healthy, or what the Bible calls sanctified through and through. Keep in mind four important facts to help you avoid making wrong assumptions as we consider this dimension of our study:

1. Seduction does not always involve personal relationships between people. For instance, people can be seduced by false doctrine, money, position, power, or any number of secret addictions to things.
2. By no means are all unhealthy relationships demonic seductions.
3. Not all relationships are breeding grounds for seductions. So don't get paranoid and start looking for a demon behind every friend!
4. Relational seduction certainly does not always involve physical or sexual impropriety.

Satan can use relational seduction to promote all kinds of evil, not just those of a sexual nature. He preys upon people's basic bent toward socialization.

In Matthew 24:12, what did Christ say would happen?

What evidence can you see of hearts growing cold in our world today? Plan to discuss your responses in small group this week.

_____

_____

_____

Take a moment to examine your own heart. Do you sense that you have a coldness of heart toward people in your life? If so, ask God to teach you how to love that person as He loves them.

Christ has called us to stand firm to the end and never give in to a coldness of heart. To Christ, loving was living. The last thing you and I are going to allow the enemy to do is talk us into protecting ourselves from relationally induced seduction by shutting our hearts in a stainless steel box. Wouldn't that be just like a bunch of humans to opt for the easy out and detach from people? Disconnection is not an option for followers of Christ. Christ didn't give His life for church doctrine. He gave His life for people. The Word became flesh for the precise purpose of connecting. Likewise, we have been left on this earth for the unapologetic purpose of connecting

- with a lost world through the gospel of Jesus Christ.
- with people in need in the name of Jesus Christ (feeding, clothing, helping).
- with the body of Christ for the love of Jesus Christ.

In terms of ministry, people are everything to us because they are everything to Christ. Our job is to learn how to be healthy, sanctified connectors. The necessity swells with the reality that a lot of needy and unhealthy folks are out there. Folks who need ministry. Folks whom Jesus loves. Lives that He wants to redeem. We are His physical body meant to flesh out His ministry to the world, and we can't do our jobs properly or safely if we're not spiritually and emotionally healthy.

"My prayer is not that you take them out of the world. As you sent me into the world, I have sent them into the world."

—John 17:15,18

In Christ's intimate prayer to His Father in John 17, He interceded powerfully not only for His first disciples but also for those who will believe in Him through their message (v. 20). That's you and me and every other believer who has accepted the testimony of Christ's life and gospel as delivered by that first ragamuffin band. John 17:15 and 18 overrule the merest thought we might have of locking ourselves within the church walls as the world around us increases in wickedness.

We've been sent to the very world the church will probably grow increasingly tempted to avoid. The huge irony is this: If we cloister ourselves in the church, we still wouldn't avoid unhealthy relationships because so many of us lack wholeness, having never allowed God to perform His work in us through and through. Here's the shocker: we wouldn't even avoid demonic seductions by shutting out the world and limiting our relationships to those within our church communities. Do you know why? Because so much of it takes place right there.

One of the synonyms for the word *schemes* regarding Satan's tactics specifically against Christians in Ephesians 6:11 is *trickery.* One of the tricky elements to a relationship Satan has targeted for seduction is that the union may not be with an unbelieving or apparently worldly individual. If Satan wants to seduce a spiritual person, he's often going to use spiritual bait. We're going to learn something highly important as we seek to seduce-proof our close relationships within the church community: the goal is godly relationships, not spiritual relationships.

What might be the difference between a godly relationship and a spiritual relationship?

_____

_____

_____

Have you ever been involved in a spiritual relationship that was not godly? Explain.

_____

_____

_____

You might be interested to know that I have heard from few believers in the last several years who were caught in a relational seduction with those they regarded as unbelievers or even those that at first seemed to be prodigal believers. Of course, those scenarios happen, but I thought you could use the eye-opener of my own case studies. I will go a step even further: many of them told me one of the very things that attracted them most was the other person's spirituality. Remember this: Spirituality does not equal godliness in either party nor does being deeply spiritual about Christian things. All sorts of seductions take place in spiritual settings. The point is not to get cynical or suspicious but to get protected and make wise, discerning decisions. Awareness of the possibility is key.

Neither spirituality nor being deeply spiritual about Christian things equals godliness.

In your own experiences, how has Satan disguised himself?

_____

_____

Do you question whether those Satan could use readily against another could be Christians at all? You may recall in Matthew 16:23 that Satan used Peter against Christ.

Read 2 Corinthians 11:14-15. What does Paul say about Satan in verse 14?

_____

What does Paul say about Satan's servants in verse 15?

_____

_____

Do you see the scriptural possibility that Satan can use believers in all sorts of ways if given the opportunity? He simply can't possess them.

One thing we must be warned to avoid at all costs is judging another person's heart. That job is for God and God alone. Judging another's heart, however, is not the same as discerning that something doesn't seem quite right and considering how we might wisely avoid opening ourselves to an intimate or close relationship in the situation. God looks upon all our hearts, and ours must be right before Him even when we're tempted to wonder if someone else's heart is right.

Stop and reflect momentarily on everything we've discussed so far concerning the world and the church. Do you see the quandary? As people who desire to seduce-proof our lives, we see that the world is going to get increasingly wicked, yet we've been sent smack into the middle of it. We can't even find a guaranteed safe haven in our church communities because relational seductions happen there too.

What's a person to do? Get healthy and sanctified right in the middle of all of it and pray for the body of Christ to get educated and do likewise! We are not going to find a guaranteed safe place in which to hide. We are going to have to find safety in Christ, hiding ourselves in Him, no matter what kind of place surrounds us. Anywhere He sends us, He is prepared to protect us. We just have to keep ourselves in Him through sanctification.

> Judging another's heart is not the same as being discerning.

2 SANCTIFIED THROUGH AND THROUGH

"Sanctify them by the truth; your word is truth." —John 17:17

In our previous lesson we looked at John 17, where Christ stated His intention of sending us out into the world, He also prayed that His own would be one.

Read John 17:23. Why did Jesus pray for unity among believers?

Dear ones, we absolutely cannot become suspicious or phobic toward one another. The last instruction you would ever get from this study is to start a witch-hunt within the church communities. If all of us concern ourselves with our own personal wholeness and sanctification, we'll find the protection we need. We'll discern through the Holy Spirit that plenty of people in the body of Christ are safe for wonderfully close, godly relationships.

We cannot allow the enemy to intimidate us into avoiding relationships. We just want to make sure we develop healthy, God-appointed, and balanced ones. We get started by becoming the kind of person we want to find.

Read John 17:15-18 in the margin. According to these verses what are we as believers to do? (Check the one that applies.)
☐ Seek to become martyrs
☐ Quarantine ourselves from the world
☐ Go into the world

We have been sent into this world. To disconnect would be in direct disobedience of that purpose. We've also established that Jesus wants nothing more for His body than our unification. We must stay connected. In both these worlds we need protection from the evil one. Christ already knew that and petitioned His Father for that very thing. He clearly stated in the passage our means of protection: sanctification.

What does sanctification mean to you?

_____

_____

_____

I do not ask that You will take them out of the world, but that You will keep and protect them from the evil [one]. They are not of the world (worldly, belonging to the world), [just] as I am not of the world. Sanctify them [purify, consecrate, separate them for Yourself, make them holy] by the Truth; Your Word is Truth. Just as You sent Me into the world, I also have sent them into the world.
—John 17:15-18, AMP

We can't get away from the concept, can we? We're terribly vulnerable in our earthly walks without it. Sanctification is the Holy Spirit's awesome work of setting us apart—purified and consecrated to God—while we're still in troubled settings. Jesus even clearly stated the process of protective sanctification. We are sanctified by the Truth.

Read John 17:17. What is the truth?

_____

We are protected from the evil one when we start allowing, indeed inviting, the Word to penetrate us through and through with its full power and authority.

Does attending Bible studies and going to church sanctify us? ☐ Yes ☐ No.
If your answer is yes, then how does Bible study and going to church sanctify us?

_____

If your answer is no, then why doesn't Bible study and going to church sanctify us?

_____

I cannot overemphasize the importance of the next few statements. First of all, much of the body of Christ exists on very little of the actual Word of God. Secondly, many of those who get a steady diet of the Word of God don't deliberately receive it (by applying it) through and through. We can get truth into our heads without necessarily letting it get through to the inner recesses of our minds, literally changing the entire way we process thoughts. Likewise, we often let the Word get to our hearts—even bringing us to tears—but don't invite it to take complete residency and authority over our seat of emotions so we can trust some of the things we feel. Further, we say the Word of God is food for our souls, but do we give the Holy Spirit freedom and authority to use it to increasingly transform our entire personalities?

On the following scale, rate the importance of the Word of God to you.

Never read the Word	Read the Word only on Sundays	Spend time daily in the Word	Meditate on the Word through the day

Allowing the Holy Spirit to get the Word through and through us instead of just to us is the kind of thing 2 Corinthians 3:18 is talking about. "All of us, as with unveiled face, [because we] continued to behold [in the Word of God] as in a mirror the glory of the Lord, are constantly being transfigured into His very own image in ever increasing splendor and from one degree of glory to another; [for this comes] from the Lord [Who is] the Spirit" (2 Cor. 3:18, AMP).

Do we really behold as with unveiled faces? No masks? No pretense? Totally unveiled for the purpose of coming to reflect the very image we're beholding? What do you think?

_____

_____

_____

Do you let the Word of God not just get to you but get through and through you?

_____

I want to lovingly suggest that if we are not deliberately asking God to get into every part of our "business," we're probably not practicing the approach that will protect us. Without a doubt, this issue has been the difference between my former and present approach to the Word of God. In the old days, I truly loved the Word and had begun to study it feverishly, but the enemy could still have victory over me because I was unknowingly blocking the power and protection of the Word from parts of my life that I either ignored or denied. Christ was only getting full reign over what seemed most obvious to this sight-impaired believer. Those old parts of my life weren't presenting me any immediate or obvious problems, so I simply didn't apply the full authority of the Word to them. What a mistake!

> The enemy can still have victory over us if we block the power of the Word.

Can you relate? If so, how?

_____

_____

_____

I wasn't actively asking God to change the entire way I think, feel, and perceive. I wasn't depending on Him to dramatically and increasingly transform me from glory unto glory. Now I'm a maniac about it. Maybe because I scared myself to death. Maybe because I realized Satan could do things I didn't know he could do. And, more than anything, maybe because I finally realized God's Word was meant for a whole lot more than I was allowing. These days I want it to the marrow! I don't want a single inch of my body, soul, or spirit to myself. Sanctify it all, Lord Jesus! It's Yours! I don't want an inch. That's exactly what the Word of God was meant to do.

I want God's Word to the marrow!

Take a good look at Hebrews 4:12-16 below. Circle the ways that the Word of God sanctifies us.

"The Word that God speaks is alive and full of power [making it active, operative, energizing and effective]; it is sharper than any two-edged sword, penetrating to the dividing line of the breath of life (soul) and [the immortal] spirit, and of joints and marrow [of the deepest parts of our nature], exposing and sifting and analyzing and judging the very thoughts and purposes of the heart. And not a creature exists that is concealed from His sight, but all things are open and exposed, naked and defenseless to the eyes of Him with Whom we have to do. Inasmuch then as we have a great High Priest Who has [already] ascended and passed through the heavens, Jesus the Son of God, let us hold fast our confession [of faith in Him]. For we do not have a High Priest Who is unable to understand and sympathize and have a shared feeling with our weaknesses and infirmities and liability to the assaults of temptation, but One Who has been tempted in every respect as we are, yet without sinning. Let us then fearlessly and confidently and boldly draw near to the throne of grace (the throne of God's unmerited favor to us sinners), that we may receive mercy [for our failures] and find grace to help in good time for every need [appropriate help and well-timed help, coming just when we need it]" (AMP).

How does it make you feel to know that everything in your life is opened and exposed before God?

☐ Embarrassed   ☐ Grateful   ☐ Condemned
☐ Ashamed   ☐ Peaceful   ☐ Healing
☐ Guilty   ☐ Unashamed   ☐ Life-giving

The news that everything in and about our lives is naked and laid bare before God is not meant to terrify His own children. Nor is it meant to make us feel guilty or condemned. These words are meant to tell us that—because of Christ's death and ongoing intercession—the healing, life-giving, wisdom-rendering power of God's Word reaches every part of us, even the deepest parts of our nature. Nothing in us or about us is unaffected by the Word when we allow God to exercise His wise and protective dominion.

Hebrews 4:12 describes the Word of God as "full of power" (AMP). One of the ways the original word for *power* was used in extrabiblical Greek was for drugs that were effective in bringing cure.[1] The word was often used as a medical term. Likewise, the Word of God applied to every part of our lives affects us with greater healing and wholeness. We will find grace and help for every need. Even those we're embarrassed we have.

I relentlessly share what I have learned about victory because I am positive if these practices will work for someone who had as much brokenness and defeat in their past as I did, they will work for anyone. God does not play favorites. All He wants us to do is admit our need and welcome Him thoroughly. I am also compelled to share what I've learned because I believe many Christians are just like I used to be. They are convinced they are allowing the Word to do its sanctifying work simply by partaking of a steady diet of sermons and Bible studies. They even love the Word. Still, they may have unknowingly practiced such selective application that some places remain unprotected. No need to wait until something painful happens. You can change your approach today!

What do you think about Bible study? Bible study to me is: (check all that apply)

☐ Boring   ☐ Laborious   ☐ Other:_____
☐ Greek to me   ☐ Satisfying   ☐ Transforming
☐ Food for my soul

Begin aggressively asking God to plow through your precious life with His Word. Don't be scared to do it! Be scared not to do it! You're perfectly safe with God.

Start practicing an open dialogue with God concerning your past, present, and future. Talk candidly to Him concerning all weaknesses, temptations, and tendencies to sin. Ask Him on an ongoing basis to reveal any area of your life that you may be unknowingly keeping under lock and key from the reaching, healing power of His Word. Approach God as your daily counselor, your "soulologist" (psyche-ologist) who knows you better than you know yourself. Not only will you find protection, you will discover a level of intimacy with Him unlike anything you've ever experienced. The tears are stinging in my eyes for you just thinking about it!

Let the Word of God sanctify you through and through.

Let the Word of God sanctify you through and through! We've got a world out there that needs the ministry Christ has assigned to us. We've got a body of believers to love and serve. We don't want to be accidents waiting to happen in either of those important fields. Let's allow God to have His unhindered way with every part of us, neglecting nothing. As He accomplishes His good work, we will grow increasingly low risk for defeat and seduction and increasingly high risk for joy and harvest.

3 CLEAN TIES

Flee from sexual immorality. All other sins a man commits are outside his body, but he who sins sexually sins against his own body. —1 Corinthians 6:18

Those of us who have received Christ Jesus as our personal Savior have received the Holy Spirit. He literally resides in us. You and I have been made clean by the sanctifying work of the Holy Spirit. He moved into us, bringing His cleanness with Him.

We have seen that Satan attacks believers in spiteful vengeance because God refused to let him be " 'like the Most High' " (Isa. 14:14). Satan knows full well that God wants to present His Son with a pure, spotless, virgin bride, so he's doing everything he can to defile her. What he doesn't seem to get is that he cannot touch or taint the Spirit of Christ in us, which is what ultimately gives us our pure standing before God. Still, we want to be sanctified "through and through … kept blameless at the coming of our Lord Jesus Christ" (1 Thess. 5:23). Thankfully, the One who calls us is faithful and He will do it (v. 24).

Satan, the ultimate Mr. Unclean, hates the fact that mortal creatures have been made clean through the grace of Calvary and the sanctifying work of the Holy Spirit. If he can't make us unclean, he will at least do everything he can to make us feel unclean. He knows that our unclean feelings can eventually cause us to act unclean. Simply put, Satan wickedly yearns for clean people to form unclean ties.

Fill in the speedometer below with your own ideas of how we form unclean ties. I've given you some thoughts to get you started.

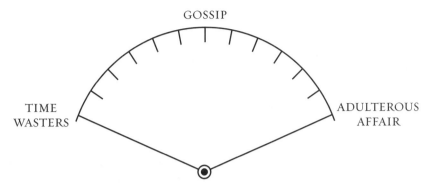

Our responsibility and powerful defense is to learn to form clean ties. Please understand a vital key for accurately applying the concept of clean ties. By ties I mean all close friendships, associations, and relationships. When I use the word *clean,* to receive the greatest amount of protection, I ask you to deliberately translate the word more widely than that which is *opposed to filthy.* I ask you to translate the word *clean* as *opposed to messy.*

What would be the difference between filthy and messy?

_____

Let me explain why our definition is critical. Many ties aren't clean that don't necessarily fall under the category of filthy. A relationship doesn't have to be dirty to be unhealthy and/or seductive. It can simply be messy. For our present purposes, we'll adopt the meaning of the word messy as the antithesis of clean according to its definitions in Merriam Webster's Collegiate Dictionary. "Messy: Marked by confusion, disorder, or dirt ... careless, slovenly ... extremely unpleasant or trying."[1]

Based on this definition, have you ever been in a messy relationship? Describe briefly.

_____

_____

_____

As you can see, the word *clean* encompasses a far broader meaning than the opposite of filthy. Most Christians quickly stereotype any kind of sexual sin as dirty, but we can find ourselves in a seductive mess that never gets physical. Let's go ahead and discuss sexual seduction to some degree first. Then in our next lesson, we'll broaden our thinking to include other kinds of messy relationships.

Remember that sexual sin can be virtually unmatched in its destructive and addictive power. Unhealthy sexuality is an extremely blatant target for seduction. We established earlier that not all unhealthy relationships are the specific targets of demonic seduction. I am convinced, however, that every assault on the believer's life to get him or her involved in an extramarital sexual relationship is seduction. My grounds for such a categorization is the Book of Proverbs, which labels the tempter to sexual sin a seducer or seductress.

Read Proverbs 7 and list ways this man was seduced.

_____

_____

Perhaps the only positive thing about sexual seduction is that we can recognize them better than some other forms of relational seduction. We must learn to form neater and cleaner ties. Please understand this: an extramarital tie of any kind has lost its cleanness and neatness the moment any level of sexuality enters into it.

Many adults are shocked when they learn that numerous teenagers equate sexual sin solely with the act of (premarital) sexual intercourse. To a staggering number of teens who consider themselves moral and obedient to their parents, anything else goes. In fact, if you are a parent of a young adolescent, you need to be very clear about what you consider the boundaries of appropriate affection for your son's or daughter's relationships. Don't assume they share your same definition of inappropriate.

While we say we can't imagine our youth being so foolish, many adults act just as childishly and irresponsibly. Countless adults enter into all sorts of sexual sin through elicit conversation, off-color teasing, flirting, and inappropriate demonstrations of affection. As long as they don't commit fornication, they rationalize that they really haven't done anything wrong.

We must recognize a radical standard of holiness.

If we're going to be protected against sexual seduction, we must recognize a radical standard of holiness. Any sign of relating sexually to anyone besides our marriage partner signals a demonic scheme of seduction. I believe that includes any intrusion into the thought life or what the world calls the fantasy life. The Word of God uses a very strong command for times when we're tempted to sexual immorality.

Write in BIG capital letters the first word of 1 Corinthians 6:18.

_____

Scripture tells us to run for our lives from sexual sin. Recently I talked with a believer who has been caught in a scheme with a neighbor. If the situation is not diffused immediately, one of them needs to move. The same is true of a budding extramarital relationship at work. If it can't be diffused without delay, someone needs to change jobs or, at the very least, departments. Do these sound like radical responses? They are! But that's what God means when He says, "Flee!"

If the believer has already been caught in the web of seduction, he or she may feel a diminished power to run. What should that believer do? Tell someone in godly authority whom he or she can trust!

Let me give you a prime example. A friend who lives in another city is on the support staff at her church. Satan began to tempt this dear Christian wife and mother with an attraction to one of the ministers with whom she worked. She had all the signs of someone on her way to a full-scale seduction and may have even inadvertently ended up being used as an agent of it in the minister's life. (He had shown no impropriety, and his activity toward her had not exceeded friendliness.)

This godly woman had the wisdom to tell someone she trusted. She admitted her temptation and asked for advice and prayer. Her confidante (not me) gave her both. She called days later with inexpressible joy, saying that since they had talked, she had felt not a hint of attraction nor temptation toward this man. The feelings never returned, and she avoided disaster.

What was Satan's scheme in this situation?

_____

How did my friend avoid disaster?

_____

_____

What had happened? Remember, Satan loves a secret! She diffused the scheme when she divulged the secret to someone who in turn helped her through prayer and strict accountability. Hallelujah! She didn't wait until something physical happened. She knew she was on her way to trouble the moment that the relationship took on a hint of sexuality even in her thought processes. You see, the lines of that tie had already become messy. She exposed Satan's scheme to the light, and he lost his foothold.

I want to suggest that relating romantically is not the same thing as relating sexually. Godly young couples who are not yet married can relate romantically with a sweet innocence, but even they need to be careful to avoid crossing what can be a fine line of relating sexually. They are prime targets for seductive schemes because their feelings toward each other are so magnetic. They have to be all the more careful not to give the enemy a foothold. He is a shameful opportunist who fights dirty … and invisibly. Establishing and paying attention to these kinds of boundaries demands discernment, self-discipline, and enabling by the Holy Spirit, but if young couples are going to be protected, they will have to be wise to the enemy's wiles.

> We must be wise to the enemy's wiles.

I am no more comfortable talking about this subject matter than you may be reading it, but timidity and lack of clarity won't help us here. Satan so hopes the church won't have guts enough to deal with issues like these. Let's prove him wrong.

Read Hosea 4:6. What did the Lord say His people were destroyed from?

_____

The Word of God has much to say about Satan's schemes against us. God never hedges from difficult subject matters like this one. The Holy Spirit applies knowledge to us as power.

Satan would do anything to counterfeit the gift of sexuality God gave to a man and wife. Nothing is any cleaner. Let's guard the precious gift we've been given. Remember, an extramarital tie of any kind has lost its cleanness and neatness the moment any level of sexuality enters into it.

Beloved, if you are in the middle of an unclean tie and caught in a sexual relationship outside of marriage, FLEE! Don't waste another minute. God will richly bless your obedience.

BEWARE OF THE WEB

Therefore, since we are surrounded by such a great cloud of witnesses, let us throw off everything that hinders and the sin that so easily entangles, and let us run with perseverance the race marked out for us. —Hebrews 12:1

I am a visual learner. Perhaps you are as well. This lesson will help us think in concepts. At its conclusion I want us to be able to diagram the kinds of healthy ties that will guard us against relational seduction. In our last lesson, we discussed sexual seduction. Today I want us to consider some examples of nonsexual relational seduction.

In the following example, circle any elements of Satan's schemes that you see.

I have a dear friend who along with her husband was caught in the powerful seduction of a religious cult. They were very active Christians who were enticed by a church that professed to practices very close to those of the early church in the Book of Acts. In actuality very few of their practices ended up imitating the early church with the convenient exception of pooled finances. They did not realize how far they were veering from the Word into man-induced legalism and bondage because the leaders interpreted the Scripture for them. They were not encouraged to study the Bible for themselves. Are you beginning to recognize the signs? They lost the active protection of the ongoing sanctification of God's truth.

In the end, this family was seduced into losing practically everything they had except their salvation and one another. My friend is one of the least gullible people I know. She testifies that this cult had a terrifying seductive power to control the mind and blind the eyes. Keep in mind that any kind of mind manipulation that draws a believer away from his or her wholehearted, sincere, and pure devotion to Christ qualifies as a demonic seduction according to 2 Corinthians 11:2-3.

For our present subject matter, pay particular attention to the following dimension of Satan's scheme. My friend said that the hardest part of the cult to walk away from was the closeness of the members to one another. Their lives were extremely intertwined. They did everything together and knew virtually everything about one another.

The separation was "bloody" because they were all skintight. Defectors couldn't simply clip the ties and walk away. They had to tear themselves away. They were not bound in the Spirit. They were bound in their Spirit-mimicking flesh. Dependency counterfeited genuine unity. Their ties were not sexual, but they were messy. There's our key word.

Counterfeit relationships can be messy.

Have you ever been or ever known anyone who was seduced by a cult? What were some of the common denominators in their experience and that of my friend?

_____

_____

_____

_____

Let's address one more example of nonsexual relational seduction in hopes that you'll have enough information to recognize the messy lines that put relationships at risk. We have referenced two primary texts in our study: (1) 2 Corinthians 11:2-3, where we are warned that a wholehearted, sincere, and pure devotee to Christ can be seduced by the serpent and (2) Matthew 24, where Christ foretold the increasing deception and wickedness of the latter days. Not coincidentally, both chapters warn against false Christs.

What did Jesus warn us about in Matthew 24:4-5?

_____

_____

Read 2 Corinthians 11:4-6. What did the apostle Paul imply about the message others were preaching?

_____

_____

In the Matthew example, Christ spoke directly to the false declarations of those who will come claiming to be Him. In the example in 2 Corinthians, Paul implied that if the Jesus others preach doesn't sound like the Jesus he preached, it's not the same Jesus! Both of these brands of impostors are fairly outward and obvious examples of false Christs. I'd like to submit to you that Satan can also seduce us with a far subtler kind of false Christ.

Anyone who becomes a "Christ" to us constitutes an unhealthy and ungodly tie no matter how spiritual he or she may be. Whether or not the person intentionally solicits dependency and devotion, Satan's scheme is to subtly transfer the deep devotion the believer has felt to Christ to a mortal instead.

Relationships we substitute for Christ are unhealthy and ungodly ties.

Help me avoid my greatest horror. Go back to the first word of the proceeding paragraph and consider this phrase in parenthesis following it: (including and especially Beth). Please, please don't let me or any other Bible teacher take Christ's place to you, ever.

Have you ever had anyone in your life who became a "Christ" to you?

_____

How did you develop such dependency on this person?

_____

Any relationship in which we begin to emotionally attribute some of the biblically specified activities of Christ to a person is not only an unhealthy tie, it is a mess. God will not share His glory with another. He will neither bless nor tolerate someone becoming a savior to us.

Do you remember when I listed the common claims of the seduced week 1? I pointed out that many caught in relational seductions used the word *web* to describe them. I found the repetitive terminology intriguing since those who used it were unrelated to one another and unaware that others had used the same word for seductive ties.

Sometimes we can still be pulling the sticky stuff off long after Christ destroys the Web.

Job 8 speaks of those who forget God somewhat like the one who transfers his or her devotion to a false Christ. Surely "what he trusts in is fragile; what he relies on is a spider's web" (v. 14). Isaiah 59 speaks of the unrepentant whose fingers are stained with guilt and whose lips speak lies and wicked things. They conceive trouble. They spin a spider's web (v. 5).

Both visuals ascribe responsibility to those who trust in a web or spin a web. Christ can and will destroy such a web, but things can sure get sticky in the meantime. Webs don't make clean relationships, and sometimes a person can still be pulling the sticky stuff off long after the relationship has ended. Freedom begins with the full admission of bondage and sin, shirking no rightful responsibility. Wisdom comes from recognizing both how webs are spun and how to avoid them. The New Testament does not use the word *web*, but Hebrews 12:1-2 offers a related image.

Read the passage below. Look for the word *entangles* and circle it.

"Therefore then, since we are surrounded by so great a cloud of witnesses [who have borne testimony of the Truth], let us strip off and throw aside every encumbrance (unnecessary weight) and that sin which so readily (deftly and cleverly) clings to and entangles us, and let us run with patient endurance and steady and active persistence the appointed course of the race that is set before us, Looking away [from all that will distract] to Jesus, Who is the Leader and the Source of our faith [giving the first incentive for our belief] and is also its Finisher [bringing it to maturity and perfection]. He, for the joy [of obtaining the prize] that was set before Him, endured the cross, despising and ignoring the shame, and is now seated at the right hand of the throne of God" (Heb. 12:1-2, AMP).

Hebrews 12:1 says that sin "entangles us." Likewise, I believe we can draw the application that sinful relationships are entangling relationships. We have discussed sexually relational seductions and then two examples of nonsexually relational seductions. All three examples had messy ties as opposed to the clean ties that protect the believer from seduction. All of them formed sinful entanglements. Whether we call it a web or an entanglement, the relationship lacks the clean and uncomplicated lines of godliness.

I promised that we would have a way to visualize and even diagram clean ties. For the sake of contrast, I also want us to diagram unclean ties so we'll always be able to picture the difference.

Draw two stick figures standing closely side by side. Then draw a rope entangling them as if someone had run in circles around them with a rope.

Have you ever been in an entangling relationship? If so, how did you get into the tangled mess?

_____

_____

_____

How can we keep our relational ties healthy and clean? Keep Christ between them! Next I use a diagram of the cross to represent Christ, the one and only Savior, standing between every relationship.

Draw two stick figures side by side with a cross standing between them.

What happens when Christ stands between relationships?

_____

_____

_____

_____

Did you notice how the lines drawn by the cross still connect individuals to one another? We've already established that we would be in clear violation of Scripture to cease connecting to others. If we'll begin imagining the cross between us and each of the parties to whom we're in close relationship, we would have a constant reminder of our need to ask God to crucify any harmful flesh that rises up in our relationships. We'd also find such peace in the simplicity of the clean lines.

Notice that the horizontal line of the cross keeps the parties connected, but the vertical line respects God-given boundaries drawn between the two. The Word of God is full of directives about proper boundaries for believers. We've mentioned three of those: lines drawn between unmarried people in any realm of sexual relationship, lines drawn to avoid unhealthy dependency on one another, and lines drawn from allowing anyone to become a false Christ to us. Certainly, Scripture cites many others, such as avoiding unequally yoking with unbelievers, but I think you have the general idea.

I love the idea of imagining the cross between my closest relationships and me because the representation means so much.

Take a moment and think through your closest relationships. Write their names below. Do you have both the vertical and the horizontal lines that the cross represents? Write *yes* or *no* beside each name.

_____

_____

For those relationships that have a *no* beside them, write in the margin what you need to do to untangle the mess and place the cross between you.

The cross offers a plumb line in our relationships.

Although we are imperfect people and we will always be challenged by imperfect relationships, I think the lines of the cross between us can offer a plumb line that can become a constant goal.

Finally, let's address an obvious question. What if we're willing to respect clean lines in our relationships, but others in the relationship are not? Then they can tangle with the cross!

Do you have someone in your life who refuses to respect clean lines? What is your greatest fear in putting distance between you and this person?

_____

_____

Take a look at the final diagram below. We can't change anyone else. For crying out loud, we can't even change ourselves! But we can allow God to change us. Our responsibility is to allow God to make each of us healthy, whole connectors and to have the courage to put some distance between any relationship that is a seduction waiting to happen.

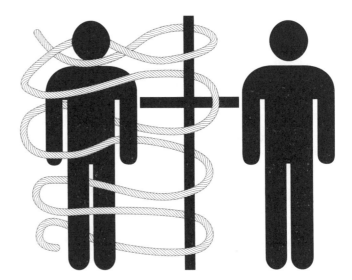

You and I need to obey God. When we do, the consequences of our obedience become God's problem and not ours. Others threatened by the change may think they are tangling with us, but as we determine to allow God to manage our relationships, we leave Christ to tangle with them instead of us. And, guess what, Beloved? He can handle them. No amount of ties can bind Him. That's not true of any of the rest of us. Give Him the ropes.

End today's study by praying for the strength and courage to do what you must do in order to be obedient to God. Write your prayer below:

_____

_____

_____

_____

5 SEE-THROUGH LIVES

Let us consider how we may spur one another on toward love and good deeds. Let us not give up meeting together, as some are in the habit of doing, but let us encourage one another—and all the more as you see the Day approaching.
—Hebrews 10:24-25

Believers have never needed one another more than they will in the latter days. As depraved as our world is today, can you even imagine what life will be like in one hundred years if Christ tarries? We are foolish and biblically off base if we think the church and individual believers will remain unaffected by ever-increasing wickedness. Yesterday's war tactics are not going to work today. Today's war tactics are not going to work tomorrow. If we're going to stand firm, we can no longer react. We must pro-act. As the world grows more depraved, the church must grow more alert, equipped, sanctified, and unified.

According to Philippians 2:15-16, what is our goal as believers?

_____

_____

Christ is returning for a pure bride who will be living in the most impure world in human history. Her purity will not develop accidentally. As wickedness increases, our only wise recourse is to increase our pursuit of God and godliness all the more. We've got to wake up and get fortified!

Hebrews 10:24-25 addresses one vital method of increasing our fortification. Read *The Amplified Version* in the margin. Underline how we are to respond to other believers.

Based on these verses, list ways to fortify ourselves as we see the day approaching.

_____

_____

Let us consider and give attentive, continuous care to watching over one another, studying how we may stir up (stimulate and incite) to love and helpful deeds and noble activities, Not forsaking or neglecting to assemble together [as believers], as is the habit of some people, but admonishing (warning, urging and encouraging) one another, and all the more faithfully as you see the day approaching.
—Hebrews 10:24-25, AMP

These verses are not just telling believers to keep going to church! Far more is implied than filling our place on the pew. Medals for perfect church attendance will do very little to protect us. We need shields and swords and the guts to help each other get armed.

I practically grew up in church and on a weekly basis easily attended a minimum of four events, yet I was the poster child for defeat. This Scripture is talking about deliberately involving ourselves with one another for the specified purpose of aiding and abetting each other's victories. Warning, urging, and encouraging one another. As the return of Christ draws near, those who isolate themselves from the involvement of the body of Christ will be at great risk for personal disaster.

God asked Cain, " 'Where is your brother?' " (Gen. 4:9). I believe God's question will become increasingly viable to us as surrounding wickedness grows more threatening.

Cain sought to evade responsibility of killing his brother by demanding, " 'Am I my brother's keeper?' " (v. 9). I think in many ways God's answer to that question is Yes, as a matter of fact, you are your brother's keeper. Particularly as the Day is drawing near.

Check out parts of Hebrews 10:24-25 again: "Let us consider and give attentive, continuous care to *watching over one another* … and all the more faithfully as you see the day approaching" (emphasis mine).

Some Christians are so watchful of others that they don't watch over themselves. They see specks in others' eyes and miss the planks in their own. That's not the kind of thing the writer of Hebrews is talking about. He's talking specifically about "studying how we may stir up (stimulate and incite)" one another "to love and helpful deeds and noble activities" (Heb. 10:24). His exhortation is about love, helpfulness, and nobility between believers. These verses are about encouraging one another and watching out for one another, not bulldozing down appropriate boundaries.

What are some ways you can "stir up [one another] … to love and helpful deeds and noble activities"?

_____

_____

_____

Since you and I and all future believers will need one another all the more as the day approaches, we need to grow in our trustworthiness and in purity of heart and motive. We have a responsibility to one another—which means we have a responsibility to become the kinds of persons who can help one another responsibly. I'd like to suggest two ways we can help one another more responsibly:

- Develop and practice godly discernment from a broader base.
- Develop and practice deliberate accountability from a narrower base.

Buy the truth and do not sell it;
get wisdom, discipline and
understanding.
—Proverbs 23:23

We've already established that for those of us who are surrounded by ever-increasing depravity, deception, and satanic seduction, one of our greatest needs is godly discernment. We can't afford to say it's not one of our spiritual gifts. God instructs us to pray for what we lack. Furthermore, the Book of Proverbs exhorts us to seek discernment, prudence, and wisdom.

According to 1 Corinthians 14:12, what are we to excel in?

_____

Discernment will be needed to build up the church, particularly in the latter days. Discernment does not mean a critical or judgmental spirit. Those are nothing more than fleshly counterfeits.

Embodied in the concept of discernment is the ability to see through what may not be completely obvious to the eye. Among other vital empowerments, discernment sees trouble, senses a warning, and cites the need for caution. One rule of thumb we want to establish adamantly is that we can't practice godly discernment if we don't walk in the Spirit (see Gal. 5). We can't trust what we're sensing in the spirit if we're not filled with the Holy Spirit.

Notice that I have broader base by the practice of discernment and narrower base by the practice of accountability. Let me see if I can explain why. One of the wisest protections you and I can possibly have is an active, deliberately formed small group of people to whom we are accountable. We'll discuss that narrow base in just a moment.

What if I sense something overwhelming in my spirit about a brother or sister in Christ, but that person is not part of my accountability group? Do I ignore what I'm sensing because that person's life is really none of my business, or do I go to them? What would I want if the situation were reversed and someone sensed something wrong in me? Would I care about my pride more than I care about avoiding a potential collision with disaster?

Have you ever been in a situation similar to the one mentioned above? If so, how did you respond?

_____

_____

_____

The rules are far more clear-cut when a brother or sister has fallen into sin, but I'm hoping to help us avoid a few plummets!

What does Hebrews 3:13 say we are to do daily?

_____

Why?

_____

_____

So, what do we do if to the best of our understanding we are filled by the Holy Spirit and we sense something is wrong with a fellow believer? What do we do when we fear she (or he) might be falling for a snare of sin's deceitfulness?

First, we'd better spend serious time in prayer! Needless to say, we are taking a big risk of offending a brother or sister, especially if we're off base. If God does not seem to release us from our concern, and particularly if we discern a problem the next time we're around the person, God may have an appointment for us.

God may desire that we make a loving approach at an appropriate time just to say we've had him or her on our minds and ask if everything is all right. Then leave the

In addition to being directly accountable to God, we are wise to have godly people to hold us accountable.

results up to the Holy Spirit. I can't count the times that I've approached a sister in this way and been told that everything was fine … only to hear from her several days later.

Whether the problem turned out to be a heavy heart, discouragement, temptation, or a besetting sin, my sister needed encouragement and lots of love. I've needed it, too, and God has never failed to bring someone into my path who discerns when something is wrong. Often God may appoint a person I'd never suspect. You see, sometimes our discernment can be clouded by strong feelings in closer relationships, but it works with startling clarity around those with whom we are a little less emotionally involved. Odd, isn't it? That's why discernment can and needs to be exercised in a much broader base.

> Is someone in your life right now who you discern is struggling in a situation? If so, write their initials here and begin to pray for them. Ask God to show you when and how to approach them. _____

Let's throw out another hypothetical situation. Let's say I have no hard evidence, but I discern something wrong in a fellow believer or in a relationship between believers. After much prayer, God appoints me discreetly and lovingly to approach the person with concern.

What if my discernment only seems to be confirmed in the encounter but he or she rejects the concern or warning? I've had that very thing happen just recently. My heart broke as I feared impending disaster in a relationship a sister in Christ was developing. I did not go to her until the Holy Spirit seemed to overwhelm me with concern and bring me to a place where I could not remain silent. I went to this precious sister very discreetly and lovingly on two occasions, but both times she assured me the relationship was safe.

What am I to do? First of all, I hope she's right and I'm completely off target. I'd rather my sister be perfectly fine than me be right. Secondly, I'm just going to have to continue to pray until God releases me, and I must entrust her to her very faithful Father in heaven.

Jude 22-23 says, "Be merciful to those who doubt; snatch others from the fire and save them" (AMP). Some people won't let themselves be snatched from the fire. Tragically, I can think of a few times someone tried to snatch me from a fire, and I thought the person was overreacting. Boy, did I end up getting burned. Thankfully, I can think of other times I received a word of caution and jumped like a maniac from the rising flame.

> Have you ever received a warning, dismissed it, and then realized the person was right? ☐ Yes ☐ No   If so, how did you respond?

We usually hear the warning whether or not we heed it.

One thing I believe I can say with confidence and based on personal experience is that we usually hear the warning whether or not we heed it. Even though I rejected a sound word of warning at a critical time in my life, I was unable to forget it, and God used it later to keep me from being deceived even further by the enemy. Likewise, I don't believe my sweet sister in Christ has forgotten that I came to her in concern. What if God simply uses the warning to give her extra caution in the relationship and all turns out well? So be it!

We are going to need wisdom, spiritual sensitivity, and spiritual sensibility like never before as Satan enlarges his seductive attacks against believers. Yes, in some ways we must become our brother's keeper, but if we are not motivated by love and encouragement, we're not moving at the impulse of the Holy Spirit. Witch-hunts or our own Christian version of McCarthyism is out of the question. If we are not motivated by the

Spirit through love, God is not the one calling us to get involved in someone else's business. Oh, God, help us to know the difference and not to use our freedom as a license for sin. We are desperate for the mind of Christ, the heart of Christ, and the direction of Christ.

A second suggestion for helping one another responsibly involves developing and practicing a narrower base of accountability. If we're going to be fortified against seduction, you and I urgently need a small group of people we invite to hold us accountable to the pursuit of godliness. Accountability partners mean individuals we invite to see through us.

Everyone from the pastor to the church doorkeeper needs accountability, but none of us can be forced into it. The structure can be placed around us and the process even demanded of us, but how transparent we are with others will always be a choice. Transparency for the believer is a wise choice. Only those who are willing to be vulnerable will experience the protection accountability can bring.

Our accountability partners are so important that we want to choose them prayerfully and soberly under the leadership of the Holy Spirit. We may find that the best accountability partners are not necessarily our best friends because sometimes we need more objectivity than close friends can provide. Those we ask to hold us accountable should be people we deeply respect and who have proved trustworthy over a length of time. (Beware of instant intimacy with anyone! Instant intimacy is one of the leading warning signals of a seduction!)

Although I am very public about general confessions of sin, weakness, and fault, God calls me to be far more specific with the handful of people He has placed around me for accountability. Several staff members and directors on our board as well as my husband and a personal friend know everything there is to know about me. The good, the bad, and the ugly. They have open access to question me about absolutely anything. How I thank God for them! Only heaven will prove how they have aided and abetted my pursuit of godliness and my protection from the evil one.

What about you? Do you have an accountability group who has permission to see through you? If so, list their names below and thank God for them.

_____

_____

The apostle Paul taught volumes about good accountability partners because he assumed that role with his young churches through his epistles. In fact, our key verse for this study implies several descriptions of the kind of godly accountability we need in the increasing wickedness surrounding us.

Read 2 Corinthians 11:2-3 in the margin and underline descriptions of godly accountability.

Paul left no doubt in his letter to the Corinthians. He intended to hold them accountable to godliness. He had a godly jealousy for their best.

Please notice a critical element in Paul's accountability approach: his desire was their devotion to Christ—not their devotion to him. God-ordained yokefellows are jealous for us to be God's, not theirs. Godly accountability is never codependent.

Paul demonstrates another wonderful characteristic in a godly accountability partner. He had the ability to recognize and acknowledge strengths in his companions in the faith while still discerning risks. In 2 Corinthians 11:3, Paul commended their sincere and

I am jealous for you with a godly jealousy. I promised you to one husband, to Christ, so that I might present you as a pure virgin to him. But I am afraid that just as Eve was deceived by the serpent's cunning, your minds may somehow be led astray from your sincere and pure devotion to Christ.

—2 Corinthians 11:2-3

pure devotion to Christ. Who wants an accountability partner who does nothing but point out weaknesses and spout warnings? I don't! I need a little encouragement sometimes, and so do you. Surely something is worth commending in us from time to time! If not, we need more than an accountability partner! The last thing Paul wanted was for the Corinthians to lose heart (2 Cor. 4:1). On the other hand, Paul was not blinded to the risks their present weaknesses heightened. He didn't just fret over the fears he had for them. Under the inspiration of the Holy Spirit, he spoke plainly and lovingly. They heard whether or not they heeded.

We need see-through lives.

See-through lives. That's what we need. Whether we realize it or not, you and I are desperate for people who can see through our lives. With their help, we can begin practicing lives of inside-out veracity that anybody can see through. What freedom! What peace! Take it from a former cover girl … and I don't mean the pretty kind. I mean the kind who writes "Keep Out!" across her forehead in permanent marker and keeps herself covered no matter what the cost. Oh, what joy those days stole from me!

While secluded in the mountains writing this book, I opened a gift my staff had tucked in my suitcase. It was a flip calendar spanning the time I was there, and each day had on it an outdoor scene, a Scripture, and a personalized note for me from one of them. The time they had taken and the affection that filled it was so astonishing to me that I cried like a baby. The tears are stinging in my eyes again just thinking about it!

On the very last day, I flipped the calendar to the final picture. This time it wasn't an outdoor scene. It was a picture of all nine of us. My friends and me. My precious coworkers in the gospel. I laughed and bawled at the same time. I sat there before the Lord marveling at the excellence of those He has placed around me, and I heard Him whisper to my spirit, "Look at the kinds of people who love you, Beth. And, yes, they really know you."

They know my past. They know my faults. They know my fears. They know my insecurities. I finally allowed a group of people to see right through me. And they love me anyway. Oh, what joy! A joy I will no longer allow the enemy to steal. Somewhere along the way, the cover girl broke free. She may not be pretty. But she's real.

The accepting love God has shown me through them, through my husband, and through many others who really know me has given me the courage to stand before thousands and be who I am: A ragamuffin pulled from the pit and saved by the grace of an awesome God. And I am no longer ashamed.

Discernment: the ability to see through the masks.

Accountability: inviting others to see through us.

Both help us see this faith thing through with integrity.

Video Response Sheet

GROUP SESSION 4

1. The Day approaching represents the day of _____ _____.

2. Toward end times there will be increases in _____, _____, and _____.

3. Toward end times there will also be an unparalleled _____ of the Holy Spirit.

4. Satan knows we will need _____ _____ more and more as the Day approaches.

5. Satan is doing everything he can to _____ and _____ relationships.

   Koinonia means _____. In its concept it also often infers _____.

6. In any level of fellowship we are _____ and _____ impartation.

7. True *koinonia* means good deposits.

8. We must _____ develop smart hearts.

9. We are never told to love _____.

10. We are told to love with

    • _____

    • depth of _____

    • and _____

11. To _____ well is to _____ well.

12. Many of us want to _____ the Gospel without allowing it to be _____ to us.

    The Greek word for "poor" is _____ which means "subsisting on the alms from others."

13. Our fellowship with _____ _____ begins with our fellowship with _____.

14. Loving well is always _____.

THE WAY HOME

This week we begin our journey home. Weeks 5 and 6 are all about helping those who have been Had to heal. Hope and restoration are available to the one who is truly repentant and seeks God's forgiveness. Sometimes we have to act our way into feeling rather than feeling our way into acting. As you begin to act on truth, the feeling will come. God's Word provides a road map for restoration if we are willing to follow it.

PRINCIPAL QUESTIONS

Day 1: How does Galatians 2:20 speak to a Healed Had?

Day 2: What does God delight to do according to Micah 7:18-19?

Day 3: According to 1 Samuel 16:7, how does God make His decisions?

Day 4: According to Psalm 27:1, we have no reason to fear whom?

Day 5: What does God's Word promise at the end of Hebrews 13:5?

1 NAME CALLING

> *"Come now, let us reason together," says the Lord. "Though your sins are like scarlet, they shall be as white as snow; though they are red as crimson, they shall be like wool."* —Isaiah 1:18

During the final two weeks of our journey together we will discover precepts in Scripture that will guide us to hope and restoration. Today's lesson will be different from the rest. It contains my story. Perhaps you can relate or you know someone who can. I ask you to read it prayerfully and then spend time reflecting on your own life. If you can't relate, but know someone who can, pray for that person and their restoration.

My name is Had. You may know me, but you may not know my new name. You may have no idea what I've been through because I do my best to look the same. I am scared to death of you. I used to be just like you. I once held my head up high without propping it on my hymnal.

I was well respected back then, and I even respected myself. I was wholeheartedly devoted to God, and if the truth be known, somewhere deep inside I was sometimes the slightest bit proud of my devotion. Then I'd repent … because I knew pride was wrong. I didn't want to be wrong. Not ever.

People looked up to me. And life looked good from up there. I felt good about who I was. That was before I was Had. Strangely, I no longer remember my old name. I just remember I liked it. I liked who I was. I wish I could go back. I wish I'd just wake up. But I fear I'm wide awake. I have had a nightmare. And the nightmare was me. Had.

If I could really talk to you and you could really listen, I'd tell you I have no idea how all this happened. Honestly, I was just like you. I didn't plan to be Had. I didn't want to be Had. One day I hadn't, then the next day I had.

Oh, I know now where I went wrong. I have rewound the nightmare a thousand times, stopping it right at the point where I departed the trail of good sense. The way ahead didn't look wrong. It just looked different. Strange, he didn't look like the devil in the original scene. But every time I replayed it, he dropped another piece of his masquerade. When he finally took off his mask, he was laughing at me. Nothing seems funny anymore. I will never laugh again as long as he is laughing.

If only I could go back. I would see it this time! I would walk around the trap camouflaged by the brush, and I would not be Had. I would be Proud. Was that my old name? Proud? I can't even remember who I was anymore. I thought I was Good. Not Proud. But I don't know anymore.

Would you believe I never heard the trap shut? Too many voices were shouting in my head. I just knew I got stuck somewhere unfamiliar, and soon I didn't like the scenery anymore. I wanted to go home. My ankle didn't even hurt at first. Not until the infection set in. Then I thought I would die.

I lay like a whimpering doe while the wolf howled in the darkness. I got scared. I pulled the brush over me and hid. Then I felt like I couldn't breathe. I had to get out of there or I was sure it would kill me. I didn't belong there. I refused to die there.

I pulled and pulled at the trap, but the foothold wouldn't budge. The blood gushed. I had no way out. I screamed for God. I told Him where I was and the shape I was in. He came for me.

The infection is gone. He put something on it and cleaned it up instantly. As He inspected my shattered ankle, I kept waiting for Him to say, "You deserved this, you know. You've been Had." Because I did and I know and I have. He hasn't said it yet. I don't know whether He will or not. I don't know how much to trust Him yet. I've never known Him from this side. My leg still hurts. God says it will heal with time. But I fear I will always walk with a limp.

You see, I wrestled with the devil and he gave me a new name. Had.

Have you ever been Had? If so, describe your experience below:

_____

_____

_____

If you have never been Had, do you really think that it is possible?
☐ Yes   ☐ No   ☐ Not sure Why?

_____

This part's just for you, Had.

All sorts of people take this study. People who want to help Had. People who want to judge Had. People who want to know how bad was Had. And people who want to know how sorry is Had. They can read it if they want, but this part is not for them. It's just for you. Had.

In case no one has said it to you yet, I'm sure sorry you've been Had. It's horrible, isn't it? Devastating not to live up to your own expectation. To become such a pauper to Grace. I've been Had a time or two myself. It's been a while, but I remember well what it was like being him.

God says He doesn't want me to forget. I asked Him why. He said too many people have been Had out there. All sorts of ways to be Had. Good and Proud think there are just a few, but if they're not careful, they may be Wrong. And someday they may even be Had. But I don't hope so. I don't wish anyone to be Had. I used to wish I could be Good and Proud again, but I don't anymore. I don't want to be Good, Proud, or Had. I just want to be Healed.

Have Good and Proud ever gotten in the way of your being Healed? Explain.

_____

_____

_____

God says He will never let me be so Healed that I forget about Had. There have been more Hads than Good and Proud may ever know. Sometimes it takes a Has Been to know a Had.

One thing is for sure. Had needs a lot of Help. Healed's nickname is Help. He got the name because he is what he does. He can't stop. Healed Hads Help.

God wanted to make sure I never act like I haven't been Had, so He left the scars. He kept a set on His own hands and feet and left one on my ankle. That's OK. My scars bear the marks of death. Don't let anyone tell you that being Had won't kill you. It will. It was meant to. If it doesn't, you've been Had for nothing and you'll be Had again.

Christ raises the dead only after they die. Before I was Had, God kept saying, "You are not yet Dead." So instead I was Had. Christ let Lazarus lie dead for four days, but not because He was mean. Scripture says He loved Lazarus even though He let the illness kill him.

How does Galatians 2:20 speak to a Healed Had?

_____

Perhaps we all need to know how it feels to be dead for a while. But do we believe we might see the glory of God? That's what Christ told Martha she would see. When He raised Lazarus from the dead, Christ did not raise Him sick. He raised him Healed. I have a suspicion that Lazarus never got to kid himself into thinking he couldn't get sick again. He just asked for Grace never to be Had again.

Come on, Had. Let's you and I go on a walk together. It's time for you to go home. Maybe to a part of God's home where you've never even been. I'll walk you part of the way, and we'll talk. You don't have to hang your head with me. Then again, you can if you want. You can cry, get mad, throw rocks, and kick at the dirt.

Been there. Just keep walking.

How do you feel about Had?

_____

_____

_____

I just want to be Healed.

What lessons can you take for yourself from today's study?

_____

_____

If you don't really relate to some of the material this week, give thanks to God. You can still read and study to understand and support some people who do.

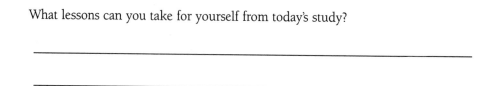

2 STARTING HOME

Godly sorrow brings repentance that leads to salvation and leaves no regret, but worldly sorrow brings death. —2 Corinthians 7:10

This week we are going to discover ways to start the journey toward home. All you need to get started is to know you need to get started. Very likely you are somewhere between having a thousand feelings and having none at all. That's O.K.

Can you think with your head rather than your heart? Can you think with that one little part of your mind that God kept covered with His hand, protected from corruption and confusion? Take a moment to describe what you are feeling at this point in our study.

_____

_____

The Truth is still in there, and He's telling you what to do. Follow what you know to be true. Do what His Word says. Disregard some of the ways you feel right now.

Your heart has been so misshapen by the twists of Satan's lies that you'd better not trust it for a while. You'll know when your heart is starting to get well. It will hurt so badly with throbbing pangs of repentance, you'll think you're going to die. And you will. Then God will raise you from the very thing that has been the death of you. He really will give you a future.

I ask you, in fact I would beg you if that would make a difference, to do several things at this point of the journey. Remember that seductions can come in lots of forms. In case your seduction is one Satan used to tempt you to leave your family or to divorce your spouse, if it's not too late, don't! You are not in any shape to make those kinds of decisions, and we must allow the destroyer to destroy no more. Don't let Satan have another inch. The first piece of armor you've got to put back on is the breastplate of righteousness. Your injured heart will be protected by your *doing* what is right until you *feel* what is right.

Satan wants you to feel hopeless. He is a liar. You belong to God. Tighten that helmet of salvation around your head. Know that you know you are His and nothing has ripped you from His hand. To remind you of that, take a pen right now and write in the margin several times: "I am God's."

Don't let Satan have another inch!

You may wish you could flee from God's presence. Read Psalm 139:9-10. What do those verses say to you about fleeing from God's presence?

_____

_____

He made a blood covenant with you, and He is faithful when we are faithless.

Because you know it's your only ticket to freedom, by a sheer act of your will, chain yourself to the wrist of Christ and start taking your first steps out of the darkness. You probably don't trust anyone right now, and you're not even sure you can trust God. You can, but you'll learn all that for yourself. No one can really tell you what you're about to learn for yourself—if you're willing.

Take a moment to express your feelings to God. Tell him about your fears, your concerns, your hurts, or your lack of trust. Be honest before Him.

Don't worry about the future right now. Just offer Him your wrist and tell Him to drag you home even if you're not sure you belong or even want to go. You do. You're just too wounded right now to feel it.

What will God do because of His blood covenant with you (Zech. 9:11-12)?

_____

I want to ask you to do another critical thing if you haven't already. Muster up every bit of the courage within you and ask God to baptize you in a tide of sorrow over your sin. Ask Him to do it for as long as necessary until full repentance comes.

I beg you not to be afraid of this kind of sorrow. The Bible calls this "godly sorrow" (2 Cor. 7:10), and it is the most wonderful thing that can happen to you in the next little while. You cannot be restored until it comes.

Godly sorrow brings repentance that leads to salvation and leaves no regret, but worldly sorrow brings death.
—2 Corinthians 7:10

Don't misunderstand. I don't want you waiting on this sorrow to come before you walk away from your darkness. We've already established that the decision to go home is often an act of volition based on what you know to be true. Often you have to walk away from the seductive clutches of the evil one to begin feeling the health of godly sorrow.

Ask Christ to come get you. Tell Him that you are willing to leave. Then ask the Holy Spirit who has been temporarily quenched to come and do His job. Be patient until He does. The tide may come in rather slowly, but if you belong to God, it will come. It must. Our Head, Jesus Christ, said, " 'Why are you thinking these things in your hearts? Which is easier: to say, "Your sins are forgiven," or to say, "Get up and walk"? But that you may know that the Son of Man has authority on earth to forgive sins' … He said to the paralyzed man, 'I tell you, get up, take your mat and go home' " (Luke 5:22-24).

Do you care about a fellow Had who is feeling a bit paralyzed? Why don't you and I remove a few tiles on the nearest roof and place him "right in front of Jesus" (Luke 5:19)?

Read James 2:12-13 in the margin. What do these verses say about the one who does not show mercy?

_____

_____

So speak and act as [people should] who are to be judged under the law of liberty [the moral instruction given by Christ, especially about love]. For to him who has shown no mercy the judgment [will be] merciless, but mercy [full of glad confidence] exults victoriously over judgment.
—James 2:12-13, AMP

What does mercy do over judgment?

_____

Read Micah 7:18-19. What does God delight to do?

_____

Why don't we exult to give mercy? _____

God exults to give mercy, so why don't we? I think the reason we don't exult to give mercy is because of fear. We in our injured flesh are so afraid someone will make a fool out of us. Ah, but I'd rather mercy make a fool of me than judgment. I will choose to believe the repentant.

Does God not look upon the heart? Does He not know what to do with insincerity? Is He not, after all, the One against whom any offense of inauthenticity comes? Will He not chastise His own? And even then will His firm discipline not be to chase the insincerity back into the abyss, so that He can delight to give mercy?

If the Bible is about anything at all, it is about God having mercy on the pitiful plight of men, forgiving their sins and restoring their lives. Christ never resisted the truly repentant. The Pharisees, on the other hand, could really get to Him.

Had, you don't want to be like the Pharisees. Better to admit where you're not and ask God's help to get you where you need to be. Do not fake a manifestation of the Spirit that isn't there. Have no confidence in your flesh. Just be real before Him. That's what He wants from you. That's what He wants from all of us.

God wants us to be real before Him.

To some who were confident of their own righteousness and looked down on everybody else, Jesus told a parable.

Read Luke 18:10-14. What was the difference in the ways the Pharisee and the tax collector prayed?

_____

_____

What point did Jesus make in this parable?

_____

_____

Dear Had, that's what Christ is looking for as you find your way back. The way home is humility. Make no excuses. Rationalize nothing. Blame no one. Humble yourself. If you don't yet feel the sorrow that you know will be necessary, ask God for it like a beggar asks for bread. Humble yourself, dear one. Come in total weakness to Him.

In the verses below, underline what James 4:9-10 tell us to do.

"Grieve, mourn and wail. Change your laughter to mourning and your joy to gloom. Humble yourselves before the Lord, and he will lift you up."

Before you get totally depressed, please realize that God wants us to humble ourselves, but He also wants to lift us up! I believe we must come to Him with truly humble hearts before He will then lift us up.

Read Matthew 3:7-8. What did John the Baptist call the Pharisees and Sadducees?

_____

What kind of fruit did He tell them they were to produce (v. 8)?

_____

Which of the following seem to be fruits in keeping with repentance?

☐ Human goodness   ☐ Love for Christ
☐ Brokenness   ☐ Care for others
☐ Humility   ☐ Pride
☐ Better self-effort

True repentance bears fruit. I am convinced that anyone who has been wholeheartedly, sincerely, and purely devoted to Christ and yet has gone through the horror of seduction will come out of it with a humility that can last a lifetime. You see, God forgives and forgets because He does not need to remember. We are forgiven but do not forget because we are wise never to lose sight of where we've been and how God has rescued us.

God forgives and forgets—He does not need to remember. We need to remember where we've been and how God has rescued us.

True repentance also bears the fruit of gratitude. Have you ever just wept before the Lord when all you could whisper was, "Thank You, God. Oh, thank You, God"? Healed Hads do it all the time. You're going to be one of those one day—if you're not already. All in due time.

Have you ever experienced the fruit that true repentance brings? If so, take time to write a prayer of gratitude:

_____

_____

I don't recommend this particular process and have to believe there's got to be a better way, but there's nothing quite like a fresh brush with the lifesaving mercy of God to jump-start your stale spiritual senses. Our human natures think so little of God, even in our huge religiosity, until we are forced to think more. Ironically, we need to come to the place where we're desperate enough to consider, "If God's not bigger than I have thus far needed and believed Him to be, I am history."

True repentance also swells grace. Reflect for a moment on yesterday's homework. At first Had was humiliated to become such a pauper to Grace, but when all is said and done, Grace healed Had.

Read 2 Peter 3:18. What did Peter the Sifted say we are to grow in?

_____

_____

We grow in many ways, but too few believers, if not offered a little extra incentive, grow in grace. Nothing is natural about growing in grace. Oh, that we would willingly! But if not willingly, oh, that we would not fail in opportunity!

Had, here's the deal. You will never be able to go back to Have Not. Proud is totally out of the question, and " 'No one is good—except God alone' " (Luke 18:19, emphasis mine). But you can go forward with what Hads can have. You can have an extra dose of humility. You can have a fresh wave of gratitude. And you can have a growth spurt of Grace. So can every other believer, but somehow Hads may be a little more likely to feel grateful. It's up to you.

3 A PATH OF HOPE AND RESTORATION

The LORD said to Samuel, "Do not consider his appearance or his height, for I have rejected him. The Lord does not look at the things man looks at. Man looks at the outward appearance, but the Lord looks at the heart."
—1 Samuel 16:7

Don't you think the we would be better off if we'd take my grandmother's advice, "folks oughter be mindin' their own bidnis"?

Why the small group of us had the audacity to sit around and discuss a brother's life, especially one we had never met, is a mystery to me. But, as our natures would have it, that's what we did. A Christian singer who had ministered to tens of thousands had tumbled headlong into a fall. I only know that because he said it of himself. Otherwise, I, like my grandmother, would have thought "folks oughter be mindin' their own bidnis."

This singer had admitted his sin, and as if the pain they all were suffering were not enough, the Christian world began casting their votes as to whether he should ever be allowed to sing Christian music again. I do declare, I think I'm about to get angry again just thinking about it. As I live and breathe, I cannot find a single time in Scripture when God called upon the popular vote of people to help Him deliver a verdict over one of His children. Goodness knows, most of the population would be condemned to the fiery reaches by now.

According to 1 Samuel 16:7, how does God make His decisions?

_____

God does not look on the outward appearance of things. He makes His decisions based on what He sees in the heart. He may set some people aside for no apparent reason, leaving the body baffled. Others He uses more mightily than ever after something we think is spiritually terminal, and the body is horrified. Why? God knows things we don't know. He looks upon the heart. And, by the way, He doesn't take very kindly to people telling Him how to do His job.

I went to bed that night very disturbed. I tossed and turned as I thought about my own tumultuous young life and how much grace and patience God had shown me as He taught—and was still teaching—me to walk on legs that had been handicapped for a very long time. I wondered, Have I come just a half a cup short of all the grace I'm going to get? Is there a limited supply? If so, I felt rather like David in Psalm 101:2 when he confidently announced to God, "I will be careful to lead a blameless life"! Then, as if he considered about how long he thought he could keep it up, he followed his vow with the words, "When will you come to me?"

I think maybe David thought he could keep it up until sundown if God wouldn't mind coming to get him before dinner. I know the feeling! I also thought of countless others who were like me and had required a generous helping of second chances to learn how to keep their wagons between the ditches. None of us had been so "blessed" with a public trial as our popular brother.

I brought all sorts of questions before the Lord. "Am I that off base? Am I just soft-hearted because I have been such a grace project myself? Have I lost my balance? Did I ever have any? I know he needs help and could really use a break, but is he a castaway in evangelical America? Or can he stay but better never open his mouth to sing again?" I finally drifted off to sleep, praying for him.

The next morning, I picked up where I had left off the day before in the novice Bible study I was writing for my class in Houston. This study would later become *A Heart like His* on the life of David. My previous day's research had ended with Saul's confirmation as king at the end of 1 Samuel 11. As only God would have it, my text for that day's study was Samuel's instruction to the people of Israel after their admission of grievous sin. God answered my question as boldly and quickly as He has ever answered me, and goodness knows, I've asked Him plenty.

Before I share with you what He revealed to me from Scripture, I want you to hear my heart. The last thing I'm suggesting is that I have some definitive answer to restoration or that my outlook is the right outlook. I am a fellow traveler just like you, simply trying to wade my way through Scripture for a few answers to some tough questions. We are not all meant to think exactly alike. The body of Christ is made up of many parts and different giftings.

I understand some must take the hard line and make it tough for people to come back again so they will not take the grace of God lightly. I do believe people in the spotlight have a major responsibility regarding the body of Christ. I also believe in discipline and have certainly been on the other end of God's chastising rod more than a few times. And most assuredly I believe in repentance, the real kind. The radical kind. Still, this side of the fence is where I belong. I would be nothing less than a hypocrite if I refused a brother and sister the right to draw from the bottomless well of God's grace and try again. I had to learn to swim in grace to live.

> I would be a hypocrite if I refused anyone the right to draw from the bottomless well of God's grace and try again.

What about you? List some personal experiences where you deserved judgment but instead God showered you with His grace.

_____

_____

_____

This section has been written on my heart for 10 years but has never before made its way to paper. I believe now that it was waiting for the rest of this study to grow around it. I am usually very conscious of a concept for a study growing. Oddly, the concept for this study came complete, God delivering the title to me in full. My Bible was open to these verses for the first time in a long while, and the instruction from the Lord came so unmistakably that I dated it in the margin: April 19, 2000. My pen still didn't touch the paper until almost exactly a year later when I knew His Spirit was saying to me, "Now." I headed to the mountains, and within a few weeks it was done.

I was much too young, much too inexperienced, and I needed the approval of others much too much to write something like this a decade ago. And, incidentally, no one was asking me. I had far more zeal than knowledge at that time, and God wasn't letting me out much. The beauty of it was, I didn't even know it. I'm not sure why He lets me out now. My teachers have already forgotten more than I'll ever know, and I still maintain that in my natural personality, I am blonder than I pay to be. I still pay big bucks to be blonde, but I've learned a few things with every one of those gray hairs I'm covering.

Over the past 10 years, I have had the opportunity to thumb through these very passages with many sisters and even a few brothers whose knees were pretty bloody from some kind of tumble. Not too long ago, God quarantined a minister of the gospel and me toward the back of a plane right across from one another. I did not know him personally, but I could tell his soul was deeply troubled. Later he told me he had made a decision of some kind that he deeply regretted. We studied these Scriptures together all the way to our destination. I was so humbled to be able to serve him.

First Samuel 12:20-25 represents some of the clearest orderly concepts for restoration that I've ever found in a single Scripture. We will give them much attention over our next few lessons. I will not do them justice, but may God take them and walk you through them with Spirit-filled comprehension. May they become a path of clarity and hope to you. I want you to know that I'm honored to serve you, Had. If you'll take off your shoes, I'll gladly get on my knees and wash your feet in the water of this Word.

Read 1 Samuel 12:20-25 to see how Samuel, God's chosen prophet or spokesman to the Israelites, responded to the people's admission of grievous sin against God. What advice did Samuel give? Check all that apply:

☐ Run for your life.   ☐ You are in big trouble.
☐ Fear your idols.   ☐ Do not be afraid.
☐ Do not persist in doing evil.   ☐ Serve the Lord.
☐ Keep serving your idols.   ☐ The Lord has rejected you.
☐ Fear the Lord.

We are not to be like the world or let anything disconnect us from Christ.

We will take each precept individually, considering how it applies to New Testament believers. We don't have to make any big reaches for application. Israel's situation was conceptually identical to someone being seduced from his or her wholehearted, sincere, and pure devotion to God for lesser—even spiritual or earthly acceptable—things. God's people are neither to be like the world and take on the habits of surrounding pagans nor ever to allow something that even seems spiritual or reasonable to disconnect us from the Head (Col. 2:19).

Added to all of Israel's other sins against God, they had committed the evil of asking for an earthly, visible king (1 Sam.12:19).

What do you think might be some ways that we switch our primary devotions to the visible princes of the earth?

_____

_____

God always had in mind a royal line among His people through which He would present His Son, the Messiah—the King of all kings. The heinous nature of Israel's sin against God was their attitude and motive. God had delivered them from the hands of their enemies on every side and caused them to live securely (1 Sam. 12:11), but what happened next?

What did the people ask for (1 Sam. 12:12-13)?

_____

What did they get?

_____

Piercing words came from the prophet Samuel from the moment Saul was appointed king. Read 1 Samuel 10:17-19. What had God done for the Israelites?

_____

_____

How did they respond?

_____

_____

> God planned before time to present His Son through a royal line.

Have you noticed that big trouble can begin when we say no to something God has provided for us and look for our own more rational and reasonable means of provision? Mind you, this king who became a misleading idol to them and stole their devotion also had the Spirit of God on him. It doesn't always happen like that, but don't forget that it can.

Thankfully, our God of inconceivable grace and patience did not leave them or us without remedy. The very fact that He inspired it to be written into Scripture means it has something to say to us. With this foundation poured, we'll begin going through each precept of the prescription God wrote His children through His prophet Samuel.

4 TREKKING WITH FACTS, NOT FEAR

The Lord is my light and my salvation—whom shall I fear? The Lord is the stronghold of my life—of whom shall I be afraid? —Psalm 27:1

First Samuel 12:20-25 provides us a road map for restoration. Read those verses again to refresh your memory. We are going to examine each phrase to see what facts we can learn about restoration.

"Do not be afraid" (v. 20).

When we've really been Had and we're beginning to wake up to what is happening, one of the first, most inundating waves of emotion is fear. I find it interesting and infuriating that Satan subtly talks people into things and then proceeds to taunt and terrorize them with fear.

Later in the prescription God wrote through the prophet Samuel, we'll see the appropriate kind of fear. All others come from Satan and our flesh nature. The enemy can fuel fear in a Had through three primary areas:

1. Fear of consequences
2. Fear of people
3. Fear of future circumstances

Have you ever experienced fear in any of these areas? If so, which ones and how?

_____

_____

Choose trust and live.

Had, you probably have never been in a position where you were so forced to trust in the sovereignty of God. You will either learn to trust Him as never before, or you will be impaired for the rest of your life. Choose trust and live. God is all-wise. He will not appoint any chastisement or allow any consequences that cannot be used for your ultimate benefit.

Do you know people of godly integrity who know how to war in prayer? If so, write their names below. If not, ask God to lead you to prayer warriors.

_____

_____

Now I want you to get your enlisted prayer warriors to start praying for you. Together start binding the enemy from any further work in your situation. Pray according to Matthew 16:19, asking God to bind Satan and to loose the Holy Spirit on every single detail. Bind it from Satan in Jesus' powerful name, and loose it to the full, trustworthy work of God through His Holy Spirit. I would even suggest that you write Matthew 16:19 on an index card and memorize it.

Read Matthew 18:19-20. What did Jesus say happens when we pray together?

_____

As you and several others agree in binding the enemy, whatever is loosed, even if it is temporarily painful, will be from heaven and not from hell and will work for your good. Every day for the duration of your healing process you are going to need to concentrate on Scriptures that speak of trusting God. Completely humble and surrender yourself and all things concerning you into His loving hands and His wise plan.

Paraphrase Psalm 138:6-8 to write a prayer for yourself.

_____

_____

_____

_____

Always remember to ask God to empower you not to let your heart melt over the fear of men. David wrote:

> "When I am afraid,
>   I will trust in you.
> In God, whose word I praise,
>   in God I trust; I will not be afraid.
>   What can mortal man do to me?" (Ps. 56:3-4).

Christ faced much more frightening circumstances than we do. What did Christ say to His disciples in such a time (Matt. 10:28)?

_____

According to Proverbs 29:25 what will the fear of man prove to be?

_____

In more public situations, you may be tempted to worry about what people are saying. You're going to have to release them and your pride entirely to the Lord. You may even have to let go of your overwhelming desire to take up for yourself if gossipers share things they don't even know.

Your responsibility is getting entirely back on track with God. Your pride will take a beating through this whole thing, but keep in mind that the sifting of our proud natures is one of God's primary divine intentions. God wants our pride not only to take a beating but a killing! Those who haven't been Had by seduction but are Had by pride are in terrible trouble in their own right.

God has no use for pride. It's one of the few things Scripture points out that He absolutely hates. Every time God steps on your pride through all of this and it yells, "Ouch!" ask Him to go ahead and stomp on it until He kills the wicked thing.

I know it hurts when others talk—especially those you truly care about. Trust God to use time to tell of your restored and growing godly character as He sifts the tares from the wheat of your life.

Read 1 Peter 2:15. How can we silence the ignorant talk of foolish men?

_____

_____

Though the Lord is high, yet has He respect to the lowly [bringing them into fellowship with Him]; but the proud and haughty He knows and recognizes [only] at a distance. Though I walk in the midst of trouble, You will revive me; You will stretch forth Your hand against the wrath of my enemies, and Your right hand will save me. The Lord will perfect that which concerns me; Your mercy and loving-kindness, O Lord, endure for ever; forsake not the works of Your own hands.
—Psalm 138:6-8, AMP

Seek God's approval with everything in you, and ask for the empowering of His Spirit not to let your sin make you a servant of men.

What would happen if Paul had tried to please men rather than God (Gal. 1:10)?

_____

_____

During seasons of fear in my life, I have soaked myself in the balm of Psalm 27. Dear One, consider doing the same.

Stop here and read Psalm 27. Why do we have no reason to fear (v. 1)?

_____

_____

Believe and count on God's Word as you never have before to come out of your season as a Healed Had.

"You have done all this evil" (v. 20).

Dealing with the evil you have done is a critical part of becoming a Healed Had.

As difficult as this part of the process is to handle, dealing with the evil we have done is one of the most critical parts of the process. If you shirk it in any way, you will never be free. Do not downplay the seriousness of any sin you have committed—either before God or before those who must know before you can get the help you need. Do not give in to the temptation to transfer your sin, blame it, or rationalize it. Do not dream of minimizing it in comparison to what you may reason are bigger sins.

For instance, if you are married and became very emotionally attached to someone other than your spouse, do not even think of minimizing your betrayal by reasoning that nothing physical happened. Take full responsibility before God for the betrayal of your heart. Take full responsibility also to your spouse if she or he already suspects such a thing and would not be further devastated by your confession. Confess it to anyone else who is absolutely necessary in your full restorative process.

If sins have been committed against a church body or a group of people, forgiveness should be sought through a heartfelt confession of a general nature if the details are unedifying. The truly repentant will not be able to keep from begging forgiveness from anyone or any group of people against whom he or she has sinned.

Seek counsel from godly people in authority to know whether certain kinds of confessions could cause more devastation than good. Each situation can be very different and applying hard-and-fast rules to them in a study of this sort would be unwise.

You may be relieved that your situation is not as serious as the ones I just described. Caution! That's exactly the kind of attitude I'm warning you to avoid! Whatever your circumstances, if you have been seduced away from your wholehearted, sincere, and pure devotion to Christ, something huge has happened, and sin has been involved. The more seriously you take the seduction, the more freedom God will have to deal with it fully and get your precious life back on track. Trust me. Unfortunately, I know what I'm talking about here.

Come before God and anyone else who is necessary to your healing process, saying without hesitation or a single disclaimer, "I have done all this evil." The closer you have been to God, the more sensitive you are likely to be to all kinds of offenses. Even if others don't see the big deal, if you have been close enough to God to know it is a big deal, you are wise to make a very big deal of it with Him and whomever else you must to be fully restored. This kind of confession and willingness to take full responsibility will prove to be life to you and the full catalyst of forgiveness and restoration.

"Yet do not turn away from the LORD*" (v. 21).*

Whatever way you've been Had and no matter what you have done, please, please, please don't even consider turning away from the Lord as an option. Remember, that's exactly what the enemy is after! Do you remember the primary goal of the seducing spirits of latter days?

Please, don't ever consider turning away from the Lord as an option.

What does 1Timothy 4:1 say would happen in the latter days?

_____

_____

Whatever you do, do not turn away from the faith! In fact, for our present purposes, I implore you not to turn away from *faith*.

What do you really believe about God? What you are going through right now is sure going to help you answer that question. You may be about to find out that some or much of what you've believed wasn't nearly enough or that it wasn't even accurate. Was your faith in yourself and in your ability to be good, righteous, and always wise? Or was your faith in God, who demonstrates (present tense) His own love for us in this: "While we were still sinners, Christ died for us" (Rom. 5:8)?

Scripture is clear that our righteous acts are nothing but filthy rags before God. If your faith is in your own righteousness, you are in big trouble. It's time to turn away from all the things your faith may have been in and trade them for all the things faith truly concerns—like the finished work of Calvary. Christ didn't cry from the cross, "It is finished all except for that thing that terrible Had is going to do in the year _____. I'll have to come up with a different sacrifice for that. Or, then again, I guess Had will just have to go to hell. This death is not enough."

Are you going to turn away from your faith, or are you going to believe what God's Word says? Read Colossians 2:13-15. What does it say about our sin?

_____

_____

Every one of our sins was applied to Christ's cross in advance. Oh, I know what's coming next! Someone's about to ask if that applies to sins committed after salvation or just those before. I do believe Colossians 2:13-15 says *all*. Furthermore, the entire Book of 1 John is written about developing a fuller fellowship with Christ, and its audience already believed in Christ unto salvation. To them and us he wrote: "If we claim to be without sin, we deceive ourselves and the truth is not in us. If we confess our sins, he is faithful and just and will forgive us our sins and purify us from all unrighteousness. If we claim we have not sinned, we make him out to be a liar and his word has no place in our lives" (1 John 1:8-10).

Let's take a faith test. Check each statement that applies to you.
☐ My faith is strong.
☐ My faith is weak.
☐ I believe only what I can see.
☐ It is hard for me to accept that Christ's death on the cross was for me.
☐ I believe that I am completely forgiven because of Christ's death on the cross.

The Word is clear that the work of the cross is finished. One hundred percent complete. The means of forgiveness and total purification for every sin we have or will ever commit and obediently confess has already been accomplished. Here's where it all comes down: are we going to have faith in God and His Word or in our ridiculously weak and sin-prone selves?

Of the three precepts we studied today, which one is the most difficult for you?
1. Trusting God instead of living in fear
2. Confessing my sin before God and, when necessary, before others
3. Believing God to forgive my sins and cleanse me from all unrighteousness

5 KEEP ON TREKKING

Being confident of this, that he who began a good work in you will carry it on to completion until the day of Christ Jesus. —Philippians 1:6

Today we continue to look at precepts from 1 Samuel 12:20-25. Before we delve into God's word, take a moment to pray—ask God to open your heart and mind to receive what He has for you today. Then read 1 Samuel 12:20-25 again. We will pick up where we left off.

"Serve [the LORD] with all your heart" (v. 24).
Here is where I may differ from some of the hard-liners. I want to speak directly not just to Had right now but to those who are meant to help Had heal. I do not believe by any stretch of the imagination that God wills for the church or the body of Christ to refuse a fallen or otherwise seduced servant who has been wholeheartedly, sincerely, and purely devoted to Christ the right to serve again. You may as well hang them with a rope because you will virtually kill them.

Yes, they need to seek sound spiritual and emotional health, and yes, they need to follow through with steps like the ones we're about to discuss, but the goal must be fully restored servants of Jesus Christ. I will not argue that the type of service may need to change, but to refuse true servants the right to serve at all is nearly to destroy them. I would rather be that person (or myself, a former Had) at the judgment than the audacious person who enforces such a death sentence on the repentant (Jas. 2:12-13).

I don't even think those who have never been wholeheartedly devoted and end up falling in their own rebellion ought to be refused the right to serve after complete repentance and an active pursuit toward spiritual wellness. Their failure may be the very thing God uses to sift them and make them true foot-washing servants.

The truly repentant are often so purified and humbled by disaster that they are willing to do anything! If persons who claim repentance are still arrogant and unwilling

God may be using failure to sift a Had.

to take responsibility, they are probably missing the fruit of repentance. They are a long way from ready, but don't bail out on them even then! Help them, speak the truth in love, and pray them to true repentance!

If returning Hads do have the fruit of repentance, make sure they know the goal. And don't wait long to use them so they will not lose heart! Make them washers of the cups used in the observance of the Lord's Supper, for heaven's sake, or give them parking lot duty (both of which have honor and dignity), but don't take away their right to serve God. That's not your right. That's not my right. It is God's alone.

In Scripture, if Christians had gone too far ever to serve again, God usually struck them dead and took them home. Just ask Ananias and Sapphira (Acts 5). If the believer is still living and bears fruit of repentance, I do not believe God is finished using them to serve Him in some way. Seek the wisdom of God!

> God alone has the right to decide who to use!

What does Galatians 6:1 say we are to do to someone caught in sin?

_____

Think of someone you know, either personally or through current events, who was ministered to by the Christian community. How did God use this individual after she was restored to fellowship?

_____

_____

Along with God's wisdom a little humility sure doesn't hurt either. The Word is clear that spiritual men and women of God can fall too (Gal. 6:1).

Please forgive me if I seem to be hard on those who have done the right thing and never fallen. I love the Have Nots just as much as the Hads. I'm just asking you not to be Had by self-righteousness, pride, or judgment in exchange for not being Had by other things that seem more wicked. Please have mercy mixed with a heaping cupful of wisdom on old Had. He really needs your help right now.

Had, don't you dare get all puffed up about this. Your job is to stay humble and to serve the Lord with all your heart with no thought to big or small things. If God wants to open doors for you to serve Him, He is perfectly capable of doing it.

The argument God used to lead me to the restorative concepts in 1 Samuel 12:20-25 focused to a great extent on the subject matter involved in this point. No Christian in his or her right mind would say a repentant Had couldn't be forgiven by God or shouldn't be forgiven by others. The controversy seems to concern what Had is allowed to do even after he is Healed.

You probably recall the general circumstances I shared about the fallen brother who led to the discussion and low-heat argument. The biggest point of contention was over whether he should ever be allowed to sing or sell Christian music again. I do mean *ever.* (As if that were our decision.) Some said, "I think he should just go into secular music now and forget ever singing in Christian arenas again."

Wait a second. And that would accomplish exactly what?

First Samuel 12:20 says not to turn away from the Lord; instead serve Him with all your heart. Likely, the very issue in some Hads' lives who lacked complete devotion might have been that they were not serving with all their hearts. Part of their prescription would be to return to serving God—but this time with all their hearts.

Then verse 21 explicitly says, "Do not turn away after useless idols. They can do you no good, nor can they rescue you, because they are useless." I can't think of a more pointed example of turning to an idol and literally worshiping it than taking a God-given gift or talent and serving the godless world with it from then on. Not only would it be idolatry; the idolatrous world would render the God-given gift or talent useless!

Not only must Had be very careful what he does; you and I better be careful what we help Had do. Again, if Had has no fruit of repentance, he's not just Had—he's still Being Had. In that case, he has no business serving in places of influence. But this study is almost entirely concerned with Repentant Had.

If you know someone who is a Repentant Had and feels unworthy to serve, please call or write them a note of encouragement reminding them of God's love and forgiveness as well as yours.

What does God's Word promise at the end of Hebrews 13:5?

_____

_____

"For the sake of his great name the LORD will not reject his people" (1 Sam 12:22). Thank goodness! You and I need never fear that God will reject one of His own.

How does it make you feel to know that God will never reject you if you are one of His own?

_____

_____

_____

Did you notice why? For the sake of His great name! You see, the Lord will not reject you no matter what you've done to your name. His faithfulness to you is based on His great name! His great name stands even if we fall! Is His name still great? The Lord will not reject you, child. Get a load of this next one!

"The LORD was pleased to make you his own" (1 Sam. 12:22).

We'd be wise to say this Scripture out loud until both our heads and our hearts hear it.

Not only are you protected from rejection for the sake of God's great name; it just so happens that the Lord was pleased to make you His own. You'd be wise to say this Scripture several times out loud until both your head and your heart hear it. If you are tender-hearted and as devastated as I have been several times in my life, some of you Hads are going to stop for a little while and bawl. Been there. I just might stop here and bawl with you. You just take your time, and we'll pick up whenever you're ready.

In case you're wondering if that's just one Scripture taken out of context and fear it may not agree with the whole counsel of God's Word, here are a few more.

Read Psalm 18:16-19. Why did the LORD rescue you?

_____

Did you hear that? Oh, take a minute to absorb that truth to the marrow of your being. The Lord rescued you because He delighted in you. He who began a good work will be faithful to complete it (Phil. 1:6).

God delights in you!

As you read the following verses, underline all the privileges that are ours as through Christ.

"In love he predestined us to be adopted as his sons through Jesus Christ, in accordance with his pleasure and will. In him we have redemption through his blood, the forgiveness of sins, in accordance with the riches of God's grace that he lavished on us with all wisdom and understanding. In him we were also chosen, having been predestined according to the plan of him who works out everything in conformity with the purpose of his will" (Eph. 1:4-5,7-8,11).

My intention is certainly not to debate predestination. I simply want to point out that the same Mind who knew in advance you would become one of His children also knew in advance you'd fall for a deceptive scheme of the evil one. Still, He says you were adopted with pleasure.

I'm crazy about my husband for about a thousand reasons. One of the things that I love so much about him is a polite little saying that he repeats almost every time someone thanks him for something. He doesn't just say, "You're welcome." He says, "It was my pleasure." Two very different things. Oh, beloved Had, please hear this with your whole heart. When you say, "Oh, God, thank You so much for saving me and making me Your child." According to Scripture He doesn't just say, "You're welcome." Hear Him say to you, "It was My pleasure."

Many times in the months and years to come as Had heals, you're going to find yourself saying, "Oh, God, thank You, thank You, thank You for rescuing me and doing what it took to deliver me from a foe that was too strong for me." And His answer will be, "It was My pleasure. I rescued you because I delight in you."

I just want to shout Hallelujah!

Did you notice, as well, in the Ephesians passage that God lavishes His grace on you with all wisdom and understanding? He's not running low. Don't miss the fact that God will work this out, dear Had, in conformity with the purpose of His will. You haven't done the one thing God can't turn around and use together with everything else in your life for good.

According to Romans 8:28, "God works for the _____ of those who love him."

Oh, how God has used defeats of all different kinds in my life for good! Some time back I wrote in my Bible, "God, there is one thing I would have hated worse than some of the things I've been in my life: what I would've been without them."

Please don't misunderstand or misapply what I just wrote. I despise some of the places I have been in the course of my life. If I had it to do all over again, I would desperately want to follow God in joyful obedience, never veering from His path. I have paid an enormous price for the foolish decisions I have made out of an unhealthy heart and soul.

The memories I have to deal with from my past can be heartlessly haunting. I am so frantic not to veer from the path for the rest of my days that I have become maniacal about seeking wholeness in Christ. I hope to pursue His sanctification through and through with total abandon, no matter what the future holds. Many times in all seriousness I have asked God to take me home before I allow Satan to pull me into another pit.

Still, I recognize I had the capacity to have been full of self-righteousness and pride. I would not have been a good choice for a spotless track record. I don't think I could've handled one with grace. Thankfully, others can. When all is said and done and we see our holy, powerful, transcendent God face-to-face, I would have hated to have been proud and self-righteous in my earthly life more than anything else I could've been. And that's saying a lot.

Today's lesson has been one that has aroused some emotion, I imagine. Whether you are a Had or a Have Not, will you read Psalm 139:23-24 below and make it your prayer?

> "Search me, O God, and know my heart;
>   test me and know my anxious thoughts.
> See if there is any offensive way in me,
>   and lead me in the way everlasting."

_____

_____

_____

_____

Video Response Sheet
GROUP SESSION 5

1. The body of Christ must grow in _____.

2. We oftentimes _____ what would be the right thing to do.

3. Sometimes we _____ a wrong to try to make it right.

4. We must learn to _____ we made a _____.

      QUESTIONS OF A HAD

      A. How could I do anything so _____?

      B. How can I _____ myself?

5. There is healing in _____.

The Greek word for "understand" is *suniemi* which means "assembling individual _____

into an organized whole, as collecting the _____ of a _____ and

putting them together."

6. If we would _____, _____, and

_____ the forgiveness of God, that would cover our need to forgive ourselves.

The original Greek for "forgiving, forgave" is _____ which comes from *charis*,

meaning "_____."

7. _____ them as you have been _____.

8. We have to allow _____ to take our horrible experience and _____

it in a river of _____.

SAFE IN HIS EMBRACE

DAY 1

The Last Leg of the Journey

DAY 2

Steps with Indelible Prints

DAY 3

Cleaning Our Conscience

DAY 4

A Stop at the Cross

DAY 5

Going Home

Beloved, we are almost home but we still have a few stops to make before we arrive. Our study this week will require us to take some radical steps of obedience. One of the stops we will make is at the cross where payment has already been made for our sin. Not only does Christ set us free from our sin but He also sets us free from our guilt when we are willing to confess and repent. Would you surrender yourself to God, withholding nothing, and ask Him to do what seems impossible? He stands ready to receive and restore.

PRINCIPAL QUESTIONS

Day 1: What are four truths about God's precepts from Psalm 19:10-11?
Day 2: According to Romans 8:1, who is no longer condemned?
Day 3: How does the apostle Paul describe a clear conscience in 2 Corinthians 1:12?
Day 4: How does Hebrews 4:16 tell us to approach the throne of grace?
Day 5: How did the tax collector go home according to Luke 18:14?

THE LAST LEG
OF THE JOURNEY

Do not be anxious about anything, but in everything, by prayer and petition, with thanksgiving, present your requests to God. And the peace of God, which transcends all understanding, will guard your hearts and your minds in Christ Jesus.—Philippians 4:6-7

We have finally arrived at the last leg of our journey. You may be a bit weary right now, but don't give up, great joy awaits you. The next two precepts in God's prescription to the prophet Samuel for His children's restoration directly assign some responsibilities to others besides Had. Let's give them a look.

Read 1 Samuel 12:20-25 again as you begin today's lesson.

"As for me, far be it from me that I should sin against the LORD by failing to pray for you" (v. 23).
I not only believe that the surrounding body of Christ shirks its duty by failing to pray for the full restoration of her Hads, but I believe Scripture implies that its sin of failing to pray is directly against God.

I am not at all a cynic about the body of Christ. I am happy to tell you that many people I know and with whom I attend church are true, humble God-seekers. They actively rise to the occasions of forgiveness, mercy, and restoration. Sadly, however, we also know the other kind: busybodies who love to have something to talk about. Self-appointed judges who love to have folks to sharpen their skills on. Insecure people who feel better and higher if others appear lesser and lower.

God uses believers in the process of Had's full restoration.

Whether we want to face it or not, we have a responsibility to fulfill in the process of Had's full restoration. Fervent intercessory prayer for sinners to be restored accomplishes several key things.

As you go through the list below, place a check mark by the statements on intercessory prayer that you have experienced firsthand.

Benefits of Intercessory Prayer

1. Prayer keeps intercessors' hearts pure and loving toward the sinner seeking restoration. You've probably noticed that it's difficult to feel lots of negativity toward people when you are actively praying for them.

2. Prayer brings the part of the body interceding into agreement, thereby strengthening the power of prayer (Matt. 18:19-20). Had needs lots of prayer! And for lots of things! You don't even have to wonder if you're praying the will of God when you ask for the full restoration of one of His children. That is His indisputable desire.

3. Prayer keeps the mouth open before God on the matter rather than open before others. We have no business gossiping about members of the body of Christ. If we would turn the time we spend discussing the other's life into prayer time instead, who knows what would happen to the glory of God! Mind you, God sees right through gossip in the name of a prayer request.

4. Prayer guards hearts and minds and causes God to bring peace out of chaos (Phil. 4:6-7). Lots of chaos can surround a Had situation.

5. The prayers of the saints to bind the enemy can ... bind the enemy! And prayer to loose the Spirit can do just that: loose the Spirit (Matt. 16:19)! Prayer can be used of God to thwart further plans of the enemy and take back what he stole.

6. The prayers of the saints can be honored by God to block further damage or destruction. God can honor our prayers to halt the continuing damage to a marriage or marriages, a family or families, or an entire congregation.

7. Prayer causes the blessing of the fully redeemed and restored to be shared and to profit many. In all the years since I was Had and after my journey to healing and a greater biblical understanding, I have had both the huge responsibility and privilege of helping some other Hads along their ways. Sometimes I've been in a primary role and other times a secondary role. I've watched high school Hads, college Hads, and more than a few adult Hads gradually heal.

I have cried bitter tears over several Hads who refused to do what was necessary and who continued Being Had. In retrospect, I can say in all honesty that raising my children is the only thing that has brought me greater joy than watching a Had be fully restored. I can hardly keep from crying as I see a Healed Had singing her heart out for the Jesus she loves more than anything else in the world. I can't keep a grip when I watch a Healed Had knock the whole place out with a powerful testimony of God's amazing grace.

Just recently, I watched a Healed Had march down an aisle in a sparkling white wedding dress, daring to believe God. I watched a Healed Had return after a long absence to teaching high school Sunday School with the full anointing of the Holy Spirit.

The list could go on and on, but the point is clear: believers who have been made aware of the situation will fail their responsibility and even sin against God by not praying for the full redemption and restoration of Had and all those concerned. Not only that, they will miss an unspeakable blessing.

Do you know someone who is interceding for you? If so, thank them. Are you currently interceding for someone or do you know someone for whom you need to intercede? If so, write a prayer of intercession below for them.

_____

_____

_____

_____

"I will teach you the way that is good and right" (v. 23).

Had, you need teaching as badly as you have ever needed it in your life. You are in desperate need of good, solid, godly (not just "Christian" or "spiritual") counsel. You need to know how to proceed from where you are now to where God wants you to go. Just like mine and countless others, your own vision, perception, and estimation have failed you. You need the help of wise others so you can improve your sight and awareness.

I cannot overemphasize that you also need to know how and why you took a wrong way. This is an extremely important part of your knowing the way from here.

Obviously, had you known what you were getting yourself into, you wouldn't have gone that way. You see, the very nature of a satanic scheme is that it is secretive and cunning. It is meant to trap the unsuspecting. You, like all the others of us who have been Had, need to get biblically educated and take a good look like never before at where and why you went wrong.

I really want to be bold enough to say that you cannot get through this process wholly restored on your own. You need members of the body of Christ, and I don't mind telling you, some of them need you!

This point is where good, godly counseling comes in—as well as solid Bible study and a fuller understanding of a through-and-through kind of sanctification. I also would like to offer another bold piece of advice. I'll go ahead and say up front; it is radical.

In Had situations where I've taken a primary role (always as part of a team), I have insisted on Had agreeing to an intense time of detoxification, deprogramming, and reprogramming. I think they are critical, and I want to explain what each means. All of these fall under the category of learning, as Samuel said, the way that is good and right.

Detoxification. Think of your present state this way: in one way or another the same serpent that got his fangs into Eve got his fangs into you. How he did it and what happened as a result differs from Had to Had. In some way, as 2 Corinthians 11:2-3 says, the serpent has corrupted and seduced your mind. I want you to think of that corruption like a poison, venom, or toxin.

In order to detoxify, you must cut yourself off from the source or sources and all connections to the source. You may really need some stiff accountability to accomplish this detoxification, but it is vital that you do.

> You need the help of wise others so you can improve your sight and awareness.

For example, if you have been stealing money, you need to get away from the source from which you found freedom to steal. If you have been seduced into Internet pornography, you must be bold enough to cut yourself off from all access to the Internet—at home, at work, or anywhere else! I don't care if you have to give up your whole computer for a while, this step is vital. You may find that you are safest never getting on the Internet again and letting others do any research you may need.

You've got to be serious about restoration. Do whatever you have to do to cut off the flow of venom. If you have been involved in an extramarital affair or an illicit relationship of some kind, I don't care if you think you're in love with the person; it is nothing but a scheme of the devil. Cut off all forms of contact with the person and also to any other connection you have to the person. Oh, please do not be foolish enough to stay in contact. Don't rationalize a friendship! Too many have tried, only to stay deceived on one level or another. Part of your waking-up process will not happen until all ungodly contact has ceased. Get all the help you need to make this move and keep this commitment. It is a big ticket to freedom!

 What in your life do you need to cut yourself off from in order to detoxify?

_____

_____

Deprogramming. However he may have accomplished it, somehow Satan did a fine job of programming your mind with lies and a lot of junk that needs dumping. Every satanic stronghold involves believing a lie or lies. Seduction involves believing a very subtle arsenal of them.

I am really going to risk getting labeled a fanatic on this one, but I have seen the process work, and I have seen the process fail. The participant's willingness to cooperate with this objective has proved to make a huge difference. For a while, you would be wise to avoid any kind of media entertainment (movies, television, books, or magazines) that encourages corrupt thinking.

Your mind will be very susceptible and sensitive for a while. What might not bother the person sitting next to you could send you into a tailspin, even a possible relapse. For instance, if you've been seduced by pornography, an R-rated movie would be extremely detrimental. So could many PG-13 ratings. I am not sure what business any of us have watching sexually-explicit movies, but Satan could use it more destructively on a Had than anyone else.

Since I used the example of an extramarital affair in the previous point, I'll use it again to keep the concepts clear. Can you imagine that sitcoms, soap operas, or all manner of programming that give approval to sex outside marriage (including adultery) would be good for someone who has already been seduced? For a while, Had's mind is far too sensitive and susceptible to forms of media that will fuel the kinds of deceptions that were nearly the death of him.

What type of media entertainment do you enjoy?

_____

List the TV programs you watch.

_____

What kind of music is aired on the radio stations you listen to most frequently?

_____

List the last five movies you have watched.

_____

What magazines and books do you have around your home?

_____

Now, using the following scale, place a 1 or 2 beside each form of media that you listed.
1. Honored God and encouraged my walk with Christ
2. Fueled temptation and compromised godly character

Please consider deprogramming from all sorts of deceptive forms of media until you are fully restored. Then you can make the decision as to whether such programs even have a place in your life. All sorts of media that don't fuel temptation or compromise godly character are available to Christians. I beg you to consider carefully what goes into your mind. Consider deprogramming from the world's deceptive forms of media.

Reprogramming. Not only does a Had need to deprogram from as many sources of deception as possible, she needs to reprogram with the truth of God's Word. As quickly as possible, get into a good, in-depth Bible study with a small accountability group. This point is essential for a Had, but it's important for all of us.

At almost all times I am taking a Bible study by other teachers. Many great discipleship materials are on the shelves now. I have so much to learn, and it keeps me under good, spontaneous teaching. God forbid that I would be the only teacher I would hear! If you can find a Bible study that speaks directly to some of your needs, that's all the better! I pray that you will consider maintaining a very active relationship with God through His Word for the rest of your life. We can't recognize lies if we don't know truth.

We can't recognize lies if we don't know truth.

List four truths about God's precepts from Psalm 19:10-11.

1._____

2._____

3._____

4._____

For all of us Hads and former Hads, we need all the warnings of trouble ahead that we can get!

Thank you for allowing me to be so bold. Please don't take just my advice. Measure it against Scripture and see if these concepts line up. Show them to someone with godly wisdom whom you trust and see if they agree. By all means, get godly second opinions! I believe they are tried and true.

Based on today's lesson, what steps do you need to take for restoration or simply to strengthen your walk?

_____

_____

Isaiah 1:16-17 says, "Stop doing wrong, learn to do right!" Doing right is a learned behavior that comes from being taught. The word *disciple* means "pupil" or "learner." We will never cease to be God's children, but when we cease learning and being teachable, we are no longer disciples.

2 STEPS WITH INDELIBLE PRINTS

There is now no condemnation for those who are in Christ Jesus. —Romans 8:1

It's time to release our fears and learn to fear the LORD instead.

Today's lesson will be our last look at 1 Samuel 12:20-25. By now you should be very familiar with the passage. My prayer is that you will apply these principles to your life as you seek restoration or grow in obedience. Had, it is time to release your fears to the Lord and instead learn to fear the LORD!

"Be sure to fear the LORD and serve him faithfully" (v. 24).

The prophet Samuel's God-given prescription began with the words " 'Do not be afraid' " (v. 20). As we talked through the first point, I told you that only one kind of fear was wise and that we'd come to it later. We've just arrived. *Be sure to fear the LORD.*

God is huge. He is awesome, indeed terrifying. He is powerful. He holds all the keys to life and death, ecstasy and agony. Our futures are entirely in His hands. He is sovereign, and He answers to no one. He holds the oceans in the palm of His hands. The lightning checks in with Him. But for His mercy, we would all be consumed. He is holy and does not wink at wickedness. He lifts up and He casts down. He makes the mind and can break the mind. When He rises from His throne, His enemies scatter. He has no equal. He is complete, pure, unadulterated otherness.

Read the following verses from Proverbs and complete the statements:

Proverbs 1:7
The fear of the LORD is _____.

Proverbs 9:10
The fear of the LORD is _____.

Proverbs 16:6
Through the fear of the LORD a man _____.

God hasn't forgiven you, me, or anyone else because our sins were no big deal. He has forgiven us because of His great love. Period. He loves us so much, He threw all our transgressions on His own perfect Son and let Him die on a cross in our place. We simply chose to receive the gift. We must never take lightly all that is involved in our redemption and restoration. If we do, we will have to deal with the Creator of the universe.

"Consider what great things he has done for you" (v. 24).

Years ago I begged God in all sincerity never to let me forget what He has done for me. I could cry as easily today about the redemptive mercy He applied when He last dragged me from a pit as I did at the time of my deliverance. His mercies are new every morning. God applies them to me every single day of my needy life, but I never want to lose sight of where I've been and some of the places He's had to come to my rescue.

I am convinced that the ability to remember past deliverance is a gift, even though some days it feels like a curse. It's worth any bad memories if I never forget God's goodness to me. I just have to remember to take any hurtful memories straight to His throne and ask Him to bathe them in His sanctifying love and grace.

I pray that God will continue to sustain an overwhelming gratitude in me and that He will do the same in you. He deserves constant gratitude, and rehearsing the great things He has done for us forms a constant protection to us. The accuser says, "Feel guilty and condemned for all the great things the Most High has had to do for you." Deliberately refuse to listen to him. The more you listen, the more he'll say. Believe God's Word instead.

According to Romans 8:1, who is no longer condemned?
- ☐ Those who follow the law
- ☐ Those in Christ Jesus

The fruit shows how we are considering the great things God has done for us. When we consider God's great deeds in a healthy, Spirit-led way, it releases a fountain of gratitude and praise. When the accuser reminds us, he poisons the waters with guilt and condemnation.

Mary's song of gratitude for God's blessings appears in Luke 1. Using Mary's song in the margin as a guide, write your own song of gratitude.

_____

_____

_____

_____

_____

*"My soul glorifies the Lord
and my spirit rejoices in
God my Savior,
for he has been mindful
of the humble state of
his servant. …
for the Mighty One has
done great things for me—
holy is his name.
His mercy extends to those
who fear him,
from generation to
generation."*
—Luke 1:46-50

"If you persist in doing evil, both you and your king will be swept away" (v. 25).

God extended complete grace and mercy to the Israelites and gave them the perfect remedy for their restoration. However, he tagged a vital warning to the end: don't persist in doing evil.

I have no idea how being swept away could apply to us, and I don't ever want to find out. It didn't mean, either to the Israelites or to us, being swept away from His parenting. He still has not given up on Israel, and I believe He will completely redeem His chosen nation through their Messiah, Jesus Christ (see Rom. 11).

God has already promised that He entered into a blood covenant with us through Jesus Christ, and He will never leave us or forsake us. Being swept away could, however, apply in many other painful ways to our earthly experience. It could mean swept away from usefulness, from the fellowship of the body of Christ, from His fellowship (which would be a fate I consider worse than earthly death), from our giftedness, from our places of service, or even from our earthly lives. God makes no bones about His willingness in extreme cases to take His children home if that's the only way to keep them from destruction (see Acts 5).

Complete forgiveness and restoration is ours—even usefulness in the body of Christ and lives of faithful service! God can work everything together for good and redeem our failures. He will gladly be strong in our weaknesses and show us His gracious favor. He can plunder the enemy and take back what Satan stole from us. But we cannot persist in doing evil. Just as an antibiotic will not have its full effectiveness if not taken under the prescribed conditions, God's prescription carries a warning label: "Ineffective when patient persists in doing evil."

God does not ask us for perfection. I'm certainly no rule of thumb, but I live a rare day without something to confess, whether the sin has been outward in word or deed or inward in attitude, motive, or omission. Remember God did not say to the Israelites nor does He say to us, "If you don't pull your act together and start acting perfectly, you'll be swept away." He said that if they persisted in the evil that got them into their mess, they would face serious consequences. The same is undoubtedly true for us. To the woman caught in adultery, Christ said, " 'Neither do I condemn you. ... Go now and leave your life of sin' " (John 8:11).

God will empower you to obey Him by the Holy Spirit within you. Cast yourself on Him if you don't believe you can leave a life of sin. Ask Him to raise up an army to help you and defend you against the enemy. Ask Him to do whatever He must do! You cannot persist in evil without dire consequences.

 Are you persisting in evil? ☐ Yes   ☐ No   If so, what must you do to break the cycle?

_____

_____

_____

God will enable you to obey Him! Claim Philippians 4:13. Personalize it below:

_____

_____

Your feelings of hopelessness and helplessness come straight from the enemy. They are lies. Surrender yourself to God, withholding nothing, and ask Him to do what seems impossible. Humble yourself and receive the help He will send as you seek it.

He who called you is faithful, and He will do it (1 Thess. 5:24)!

3 CLEANING OUR CONSCIENCE

"If the Son sets you free, you will be free indeed." —John 8:36

Torment. That's the best word I know to describe the fiery darts of accusation impaled in the bull's-eye of the unrelieved conscience. Once we've allowed and believed God to cleanse our consciences, Satan loses the bull's-eye and can only hope to hit a nerve where our pasts are concerned. As long as the conscience is not clear, however, he isn't left to hope. He has a virtual certainty. His drill points straight into the nerve where it hisses unmercifully and exposes us to the agony of unrelenting shame.

What may be news to many theologically (though not experientially) is that we can sincerely confess our sin and even turn from the sin yet still die a thousand deaths at the stab wounds of a guilty conscience. We often take God our confessions for forgiveness but not our consciences for cleansing. In so doing we leave them to the unmerciful "accuser of our brethren" (Rev. 12:10, KJV).

We need to take our consciences to God for cleansing.

Have you repented of sin and still struggled with a guilty conscience? ☐ Yes ☐ No
If so, how has your guilty conscience affected you?

_____

_____

A guilty conscience that precedes sincere repentance is the conviction of the Holy Spirit. A guilty conscience following sincere repentance is condemnation that is not coming from God. But until we've settled the matter by faith with God, our consciences constitute an invitational tournament for the devil.

God is the only One who can purify a conscience that has become a playground for accusation. A cleansed conscience can and should be received at the time of our repentance, but often our unrecognized unbelief blocks reception.

A troubled conscience respects no one. The unredeemed can certainly still suffer from a guilty conscience, which can often be the work of the Holy Spirit to draw them to repentance and salvation. Sadly, they have no real and lasting remedy without Christ.

Obviously, the lost aren't the only ones who can deal with painful consciences. Believers who walk willingly into a season of rebellion can also bear the pangs of a guilty conscience.

If you can imagine the pain of either of the two preceding examples, can you fathom the anguish of those with wholehearted, sincere, and pure devotion to Christ who were seduced into a season of ungodliness? Torment. Until they allow God to deliver them from a guilty conscience, they are the objects of untold torture.

So often our lack of cooperation with God to finish what He started defaults us to unknowingly cooperate with the enemy of our souls. Those who remain lost will have all of eternity for torment. Satan knows that the only torment you and I will ever receive is that which he deals out to us on this earth. We do not have to cooperate with him, but we do have to cooperate with God if our consciences are going to be free from torment. I hope to be able to share with you how.

I want us to study the conscience from a biblical perspective and discover how it can really—and lastingly—be cleansed. The Greek word for *conscience* in the primary biblical text I will be using is *sundeidesis,* defined by one source as: "to be one's own witness, one's own conscience coming forward as witness. It denotes an abiding consciousness whose nature it is to bear inner witness to one's own conduct in a moral sense. It is self-awareness. Particularly, a knowing of oneself, consciousness."[1] I hope you caught the concept of our own consciences coming forward as a witness.

The Word of God teaches us that Christ is our advocate and He pleads our case before God, the righteous Judge. Once we repent of our sins, Christ not only serves as our counselor/attorney; He also files the most glorious legal brief in the universe. He declares that all punishment and payment of fines for our crimes have been met.

You and I both know that we often still suffer from a guilty conscience even after sincere repentance, so what has gone wrong? The body of Christ suffers terribly from unbelief. We often do not accept and believe the full work of God's redemption. In fact, our own consciences will go so far as to come forward as a witness—listen carefully—for the *prosecution* rather than the defense.

One of the most powerful names I've ever heard given to the conscience is *recorder.* As in tape recorder. That ought to make plenty of sense to any of us who know the agony of our minds rewinding and replaying an old tape incessantly. Rewind. Play. Rewind. Play. Rewind. Play. Rewind. Play. Torment.

What does it feel like to have your conscience replaying a tormenting scene?

_____

_____

We keep waiting for the tape to wear out, but it never does. Some of us are still harboring such old guilt that it's an eight-track, for crying out loud. There is a remedy. We'll discover that cure after we compile some vital facts offered by Scripture on the topic of conscience. The Word of God equips us with at least five facts about the conscience:

1. People with a guilty past can still enjoy a clear conscience.
Praise God! I hope you'll be blessed to know that the person God chose to say more about the conscience than anyone else in the entire Bible is the apostle Paul.

How appropriate! I don't know of a person in the entire New Testament who had more grounds for harboring guilt. By his own admission, Paul zealously persecuted Christians, seeing to their imprisonments and even to some of their deaths. He considered himself to be the least of the apostles and the chief of sinners, and yet God had completely purified his conscience—just as He can cleanse any of ours, no matter how heinous the sin.

2. Good deeds cannot accomplish a clear conscience.

Referring to the veil separating the people of Israel from the Holy of Holies, what does Hebrews 9:9 say cannot clear the conscience?

_____

_____

They still can't. We can lavishly offer gifts of talents, time, money, and make untold sacrifices, but we still won't be able to clear our own consciences. The most well-meaning Hads can devote themselves to a life of poverty and perpetual good works, but they still won't be able to secure a clean conscience.

What are some gifts you have tried to offer that didn't clear your conscience?

_____

_____

_____

Trying to earn our right to be forgiven constitutes nothing but dead works. So does attempting to make sure God never regrets forgiving and restoring us by doing all sorts of good things following our failure. More dead works. We're going to find out that all we can do to secure a clean conscience is to receive the work that He's already done.

> A clean conscience comes by accepting the work God has already done.

3. The Holy Spirit works with the believer's conscience.

In Romans 9:1-2, how did the apostle Paul say his conscience was confirmed?

_____

Paul took God at His Word, and his conscience confirmed the work of the Holy Spirit in him. While the believer's conscience and the Holy Spirit are most assuredly not synonymous, the Holy Spirit works with the conscience.

God desires that we become spiritually healthy enough through faith to have a conscience that rightly interprets the work of the Holy Spirit. A continued guilty conscience following sincere repentance can be the Holy Spirit's way of telling us that we have not allowed or believed God to complete a desired work in us.

4. The conscience is an indicator, not a transformer.

On its own, the conscience has no power to change us. In fact, without submitting to the authority and agreement of the Holy Spirit, it can often do little more than condemn and mislead us. The Spirit of God released to dwell richly through the Word of God is the only One who can completely transform a defeated life. He alone applies the abundant power not only to recognize the right thing but to do it!

5. The conscience can be seared.

This biblical fact ought to scare us half to death. You may recall the Scripture we cited earlier in our study describing those the enemy can effectively use to seduce believers in all manner of demonic doctrines. First Timothy 4:2 says, "Such teachings come through hypocritical liars, whose consciences have been seared with a hot iron."

Those willing to do a study like this are likely not the ones with seared consciences, but you and I need to receive a huge heads up about the possibility anyway. Something is terribly wrong if we can continue in sin and hypocrisy without a guilty conscience. We want to have sorrow for sin! Our sorrow leading to repentance is the way the Holy Spirit bears witness that we belong to God. If you don't have it, the Spirit of God may not be dwelling in you, and you may not have salvation.

What does 2 Corinthians 13:5 encourage us to do?

_____

If we know that we are "in the faith" but we start noticing that our conscience seems to be more callous when we sin and haven't repented, we have somehow distanced ourselves from God, and we're risking disaster. If this is you, call upon the Lord with all your might and ask Him to show you what is wrong. Seek godly counsel and the filling of the Spirit who brings sorrow that leads to repentance.

See if you can remember the five facts you just learned and write them below. If you have trouble remembering, you have the teacher's permission to peek!

1. _____

2. _____

3. _____

4. _____

5. _____

DEFINING A CLEAN CONSCIENCE

With these five facts as a foundation, let's see if we can biblically define a clean conscience before we consider how to receive one. How does the apostle Paul describe a clear conscience in 2 Corinthians 1:12?

_____

_____

_____

Sanctification and sincerity are necessary for a clean conscience.

I see two critical elements that must be present if we're going to live day to day with the joy and relief of a clean conscience: sanctification (holiness) and sincerity.

1. Pursue and practice the sincere and sanctified life in the world.
This means behaving consistently whether we're in the world or in the church. Believers experience much guilt from practicing the chameleon life of environmental adaptation. We only find relief when we ask God to invade our life and personality so fully that we become the same person at the shopping mall or restaurant that we are at church.

Stated another way, something is wrong if our coworkers would be shocked to learn that we go to church. Most believers don't work in environments where preaching to coworkers is part of their job description, but would coworkers find our behavior inconsistent with our professed belief system at church? Consistency is a tremendous relief and a vital component in a clean conscience.

Let's do a little personal examination. If your name were to come up in a conversation, how would others describe you?

_____

_____

Do people see you the same out in the world as they see you at church?

_____

2. Pursue and practice the sanctified life in our relations with other Christians.

Notice the apostle Paul said, "Especially in our relations with you" (2 Cor. 1:12). Oh, Beloved, we've got to get real. We play so many games at church and in our religious life! We are caught in such a trap. Our masquerades are so important to us that we let them talk us into choosing misery over liberty. We don't get the help we need at church because so few are willing to admit they have ever had a problem.

Oh, God help us! Freedom flows like a waterfall from heaven when we surrender our lives to total authenticity before God and before others, particularly those at church.

Had, allow me to really speak straight to you for a moment. God will immeasurably bless your life if you are willing to get real and not act as if you've never been Had. In fact, He may grace your future with a greater harvest than your past if you're willing to be real.

I don't think being real necessitates telling every detail of your departure, especially if it tears down rather than edifies the body of Christ. I do think former Hads should never claim to be more than former Hads who have known the mercy and restoration of God. When all is said and done and you have experienced healing and consistent victory, tell what you've learned! Testify! Our churches, our neighborhoods, and our workplaces are full of Hads who are dying for a little hope and a way out!

I love Paul's words in 1 Corinthians 4:4. Write this verse in your own words.

_____

_____

_____

This verse states such an important part of my own personal testimony. Let me assure you, I have not been innocent. For heaven's sake, I don't remember ever getting a chance to be innocent! My innocence was stolen from me so early that I don't even know how innocence feels.

As if my victimization were not enough, I then responded wrongly, heaping sin upon sin and defeat upon defeat. No, I have not been innocent. But I can tell you this: my conscience is clear. I cannot write those words without wavering between wanting to cry like a baby and shout hallelujah!

Had, you are not innocent either, but you too can have a clear conscience. We'll discover how in our next lesson.

We need to get real before God.

137

4 A STOP AT THE CROSS

May I never boast except in the cross of our Lord Jesus Christ, through which the world has been crucified to me, and I to the world. —Galatians 6:14

Hear this testimony, Had. I have allowed and believed God to cleanse my conscience from all my past sins, and they were huge by anyone's standards. That's how I know you can have a clean conscience, too. Now let's see how.

Read and meditate on the transforming and freeing words of Hebrews 10:19-23. Who is the writer addressing?

_____

Let us draw near to God with a sincere heart in full assurance of faith, having our hearts sprinkled to cleanse us from a guilty conscience and having our bodies washed with pure water.

—Hebrews 10:22

The writer addressed believers in Christ who obviously still had need of cleansing from a guilty conscience. Praise God! I'm so glad I wasn't the only one! And, Had, neither are you! So, what are the biblical steps to a fresh, clean conscience?

1. Believe what God has already done for you.
The way has already been paved by the blood of Jesus. The curtain that separated us from God has been ripped from top to bottom by the tearing of the precious flesh of Jesus Christ.

2. Go into the Holy of Holies without delay, and take your heavy conscience.
In other words, approach God with every ounce of baggage weighing down your conscience. Hebrews 10:22 says, "Let us draw near." Hebrews 4:16 even tells us that because Christ has gone before us, we can leave our shame and timidity behind as we come.

How does Hebrews 4:16 tell us to approach the throne of grace?

_____

According to this verse, what will we receive?

_____

3. Approach God with absolute sincerity and repentance.
Hebrews 10:22 says, "Let us draw near to God with a sincere heart." Spill the beans. Tell Him exactly what is bothering you and why you think your conscience is still gnawing at you. If you realize your hang-up is unbelief, confess it as sin. Take no pride with you to His altar.

If you realize you've never repented of the sin, repent with all your might. Pour out your heart before God. He is a refuge for you (Ps. 62:8). He will neither reject you nor forsake you. He's been waiting for you to come to Him for relief. He knows better than you do that a guilty conscience will hinder you from pressing on to take hold of what Christ Jesus holds for you (Phil. 3:12).

Get every bit of sin and guilt out of your system. Play the old tape for Him by telling Him all about what you feel and can't seem to release. Let Him hear what you keep hearing in your own mind, heart, or conscience. Withhold absolutely nothing.

4. Now, ask God to cleanse your conscience just as His Word says.

Notice the words, "having our hearts sprinkled to cleanse us from a guilty conscience" (Heb. 10:22). These words can draw two different visuals from the context of the Israelites in the time of the Old Testament tabernacle.

The most obvious appears in Leviticus 16:15-16. How did the high priest make atonement for the people's sin?

_____

_____

Our atonement, of course, was accomplished by the blood sacrifice of the perfect Lamb of God. The second visual appears in a startling sprinkling of the blood in Exodus 24.

Read Exodus 24:3-4. After Moses told the people the Lord's words and laws, what did they say?

_____

_____

I think the more Moses wrote, the more he reconsidered everything the Israelites just vowed they would do, and the more he realized they didn't have a chance of complete obedience. The next thing we are told in Scripture is that "[Moses] got up early the next morning and built an altar at the foot of the mountain and set up twelve stone pillars representing the twelve tribes of Israel. Then he sent young Israelite men, and they offered burnt offerings and sacrificed young bulls as fellowship offerings to the LORD. Moses took half of the blood and put it in bowls, and the other half he sprinkled on the altar. Then he took the Book of the Covenant and read it to the people. They responded, 'We will do everything the LORD has said; we will obey.' Moses then took the blood, sprinkled it on the people and said, 'This is the blood of the covenant that the LORD has made with you in accordance with all these words' " (Ex. 24:4-8).

Can you even imagine? The people of Israel had just promised to obey anything God commanded them when Moses put his hands in a bowl of blood and began to splatter them with it. Can you picture their faces? They must have been appalled, yet do you see the consistency of God's redemptive plan? All acceptance and approach to God is based on the blood of the sacrifice. I believe Moses' actions demonstrated that the blood (which foreshadowed Christ's own) was the basis of their covenant relationship with God. They were powerless to keep the letter of the law—just as we are.

You and I realize that the blood Christ shed on the cross is the means of remission for our sins. But Hebrews 10:22 says it is also the means for the complete cleansing of the consciences of those who already know Christ.

On the Day of Atonement, not only was blood sprinkled on and in front of the mercy seat; it was also sprinkled at the altar of sacrifice (described in Lev. 16:19). In fact, the high priest sprinkled the blood seven times. Seven is the number of completion or perfection in the Word of God. I believe this act foreshadowed the perfect sacrifice for sin offered centuries later when Christ gave His life on the cross.

Remission means "to send away." In remitting our sins God takes them from us and places them on the sacrifice Lamb.

Pray through the next six paragraphs. Write your sins below the cross as you spend time with the Father in prayer. Visualize what Christ did for you by adding drops of blood sprinkling over your sins.

I am asking you now to enter into a time of intense prayer and intimacy with God, telling Him how much you want to be free of your load of guilt and how desperate you are to receive a clean conscience. Ask Him to take you back to the cross (through prayer), where you first received your salvation.

This time you are not going for salvation. You are approaching the cross to have your conscience sprinkled clean. Several of the writers of both Old and New Testament Scripture talked about God taking them somewhere in spirit. I am not implying anything mystical or unsound. I am simply suggesting that you ask God to take you in a sense in your spirit through prayer and meditation back to the cross of His precious Son. In every way, the cross was indeed the fulfillment of the altar of sacrifice.

Through prayer, ask God to take you back to the scene of Calvary and help you draw so close to Christ's cross that you can picture the blood from His wounded head sprinkling directly upon your heart.

Imagine the cross of Christ for a moment. By the time Christ gave up His life, His head would have hung forward. Victims of crucifixion ordinarily died from asphyxiation because they could no longer hold back their shoulders and hold up their heads. As Christ gave up His life for your sins and mine, the blood would have dripped from His wounded head over the thorns from His crown.

The crown of thorns was a part of cruel Roman sport. To me the thorns are especially significant because they were the sign of the curse of sin upon the earth (Gen. 3:18). When Christ wore the crown of thorns, I believe it depicted His wearing the curse of sin upon the earth. When the blood dripped from the thorns onto the ground in front of His cross, it accomplished the perfect sprinkling of blood in front of the true altar of sacrifice.

Imagine standing near the foot of Jesus' cross. Spiritually speaking, allow the blood that fell from Christ's wounded head to sprinkle afresh upon your heart, mind, and soul, cleansing you from a guilty conscience. Confess your wrongdoing as I have confessed mine. Tell God your need. Spend time with Him there.

5. Approach God with a full assurance of faith.

Hebrews 10:22 says, "Let us draw near to God with a sincere heart in full assurance of faith, having our hearts sprinkled to cleanse us from a guilty conscience." Beloved, God is more than willing to cleanse us from the guilt of repented sin! On the basis of Christ's accomplished work on Calvary, He will never turn us down as we approach Him.

For us to personally apply the accomplished work, however, we've got to approach Him with a full assurance of faith. In other words, we've got to believe God will do what He says He will do! Christ has already done the work, but we receive it by our faith. Christ came for the express purpose of forgiving sin and cleansing us from all unrighteousness. He wants nothing more than to give you and me the grace gift of a fresh, clean conscience with which to enjoy our full redemption, but we must believe Him. Hebrews 10:23 says, "He who promised is faithful." You and I must hold on unswervingly to what our faithful God has promised.

We've got to believe God will do what He says He will do!

Trust me on this one: Satan has gotten a lot of mileage from your guilty conscience. He's not going to want to give it up as his playground. When he comes back to accuse you, you are going to have to hold on unswervingly to what God has told you in His Word. The blood Christ shed upon the cross not only extended remission for your sins, it bought you a clean conscience from all repented sin. By faith you must apply and hold tightly to what the cross of Christ afforded you.

6. Record every bit of this process over the old tape.

In our last lesson we compared the conscience to a tape recorder. We talked about how many of us wish the old mental tape recordings would wear out. Sadly, people die with old tapes still rewinding and playing in their minds and haunting their consciences.

You see, the tape is established in our memory. We have no way of getting rid of it. We make promises such as, "Today I'm not going to think about this part of my past or my old sin a single time." We even make the commitment to God in prayer. Then by 10:00 a.m., the old mental habits kick back in; we involuntarily push rewind and play again. You see, no amount of determination or even time can make a powerful old tape cease playing on the recorder of our minds and consciences.

What is the answer? We have to record over the old tape with the truth of God's Word and the testimony of His fresh work! I cannot take back my past sins, but I can allow God to forgive me, restore me, redeem every mistake I've made, and cleanse my guilty conscience. Thereby, through the power of the Holy Spirit, my past is reframed, and its destructive power is diffused.

Make a new recording over those old tapes!

When Satan comes back to taunt me, I replay the old tape with the new recording of God's forgiveness and redemption on it. I have said to the accuser, "You're right about one thing only. I did commit that sin, but God has graciously forgiven me. He has empowered me to live differently and even redeemed my mistakes. He has used my past experiences to make me compassionate and merciful. You cannot make unclean what my God has made clean. I've been to the cross and trusted Christ not only to save me from my sins but to cleanse my guilty conscience. You're too late, devil. You no longer have grounds to torment me. Your voice is strong and loud, but I refuse to believe you. I believe God, and I will hold unswervingly to the work He has accomplished in me."

I just demonstrated what it sounds like when we push rewind and play the old tape with new information recorded on it. Satan hates to hear our testimonies of God's redemption so much that if you'll keep reframing it with God's truth every time the devil accuses you, he will stop.

Take your own example of something Satan uses to accuse you and write your new response.

_____

_____

_____

Oh, Beloved, let's cease cooperating with the enemy and start cooperating with our faithful God. He hates to see us in torment. We don't have to suffer an agonizing conscience when we've turned from sin! Too often we refuse to believe the cross is strong enough to cleanse our consciences! Go back to the cross where you first believed, and believe your Savior to set you free not only from your sin but from your guilt.

Let's look at one last step to a fresh, clean conscience:

7. Where possible and appropriate, make amends or restitution.

I strongly encourage you to receive sound godly counsel from someone you trust on this point. We never want to unload our guilt at the cost of someone else's unnecessary devastation. Often, however, those whom we have wronged are aware of our transgression. Sometimes we don't feel released from a past sin we've confessed and turned from because God desires for us to follow through by asking another's forgiveness or by righting a wrong.

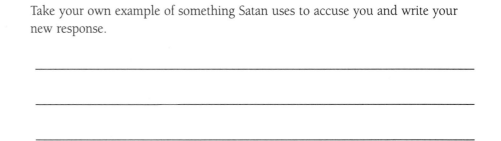

The proud will never be free.

One thing I learned without a doubt while writing *Breaking Free* is that the proud will never be free. Not ever. Liberty depends on humility. The process of having my mind, soul, and heart completely cleaned out and sanctified by God has been long but incomparable in my personal journey. My sins have been great, so God has required much of me. Redemption is due to God's work and not ours, but I can assure you that I have had to humble myself and ask forgiveness of a number of people. In some situations, my flesh wanted to follow up with the words, "And you owe me a huge apology! Your sin against me was worse than my sin against you!"

It's all sin, Beloved. And I can tell you in retrospect that I am so glad God would not allow me to do anything less than go all the way to the line in obedience. The grace-harvest has been tremendous.

God required me to approach others expecting (and sometimes getting) nothing in return. He simply said, "Child, you go and ask forgiveness, taking full responsibility for your sin. Ask any way you might be able to make up for what you have done, then if I confirm it, do it."

The more I concentrated on the log in my own eye and quit searching for the speck in others, the easier the process got. I am free today. Hallelujah! God has sovereignly ordained, however, that my freedom is not enough. I want you to be free too.

Do you need to go to someone to make amends or restitution? If so, write their initials here.

_____

Will you please do whatever it takes? Oh, Beloved, it is so worth it. Christ is so worth it. He will grace you in ways you never dreamed possible. The work of the cross still stands! Go, Beloved, and have your heart sprinkled!

Blessed relief!
    I choose to believe.
I hold without swerving
    to what I've received.
God who has promised
    is faithful to me.
Blessed relief!
I choose to believe.

5   GOING HOME

"He got up and came to his father. But while he was still a long way off, his father saw him, and felt compassion for him, and ran and embraced him, and kissed him." —Luke 15:20

Thank you, Beloved, for sharing this journey with me. I realize that it has been extremely painful for some. My prayer as we approach the end of our journey is that you will find the healing, freedom, and joy that only Christ can bring.

Dear, dear Had, this is where I stop and you go on without me. That's your Father's house over there. Many people can walk beside you on your road to restoration, but no one can take you that last quarter mile to your Father's arms. No person can go there but you, and you will never be healed until you do.

Oh, you might appear to others to have pulled it together. You might never fall for another seduction. You might go forward with more humility than you've ever had. You might serve with more purity of heart than you knew a mortal could have. But you will not be healed. Before we go our separate directions, sit down with me for a few minutes on the side of this hill overlooking your Father's property. I want to tell you why. The answer is woven like a strand of golden yarn in a wayward son's robe.

You were expecting the prodigal's story, weren't you? Surely no book on Christian restoration would be complete without it. Strange that it's the most well-known, even well-loved, account of the wandering child's return to God, yet it may very well be the least personally experienced. Oh, plenty of prodigals go home, but that's not enough to heal their infected wounds.

> Only going home is not enough to heal our wounds.

Had, I don't want you just to read this story or commit it to lifelong memory. I want you to leave your footprints all over its pages and live every last bit of it. Forget your familiarity with this story and forget everyone else who has ever referred to it. You've got an appointment with God.

As you read, picture every word. Try to visualize your Father's expression when you saddle up your beast of deception, jump on its back, and leave the safety of home. Imagine the initial exhilaration of leaving your former bounds. Reflect on every single action you took outside those bounds. Then for a moment relive the spiral descent and the sickness of a growing awareness. Feel the fear. Remember the terrible pangs of insatiable hunger. Remember the depths. Then, recapture the call of your soul to go home.

This is your story. Until you let go of every other lifeline and throw yourself into it, you will remain bound, not by your seduction but by your self-punishment.

Stop here, turn in your Bible, and read Luke 15:11-32. In what ways can you relate to the prodigal son?

_____

_____

_____

Oh, Had, do you remember? When you realized you had been deceived and had made a terribly foolish decision, did you try to glue yourself to one of the citizens of that distant land to help you? And they couldn't help, could they? Did a counselor or a friend tell you nothing was wrong with you and then send you to feed hogs?

You will find plenty that will help you stay right where you are, but the compass in your soul is telling you that you don't belong there. The only way out is home. A true son can stay in the distance only so long until an overwhelming hunger that no one can satisfy begins to gnaw at his soul.

Going home as a servant instead of a child won't work.

Do you want to go home but, like the prodigal, would you feel better about the whole thing if you just went back as a servant instead of a son? It will never work. Thousands do it, but it never brings relief. They work maniacally trying to make up to God for what they've done. " ' "I am no longer worthy to be called your son" ' " (Luke 15:19).

They never were. They just never knew. They'd feel better if they could just take a beating like a runaway slave returned to the taskmaster. Don't you realize, Had, you've already had a beating?

Oh, I see. You just want to pay some kind of penance for what you've done. Ah, still too much ego.

How is self-punishment a form of ego?

_____

_____

When will we get it through our heads that our penance has already been paid? It's pretty humiliating to our pitiful egos that the only way we can come home is just to stand right there, receive, and let the Father party over us. We still want to make this thing all about us, don't we? Well, the good news flash is that it's not.

When you're restored, if you're truly restored, you'll be free of the most seductive yoke of all—every ounce of confidence you have ever had in your flesh.

Do you think God is going to restore you in ways that let you be proud of your hard work? Nope. It's not going to happen that way.

Sure, you've got a lot of work to do so you can allow the Holy Spirit to sanctify you through and through and fortify you against ever riding another beast of deception off your Father's property. So did I. But restoration? God does that all by Himself. You just have to stand there as humbled as you've ever been in your life and come face-to-face with grace. When all is said and done, the only boasting you'll have left is that of a certain former murderer and relentless persecutor who enjoyed more freedom in Christ than the best of the apostles:

"May I never boast except in the cross of our Lord Jesus Christ, through which the world has been crucified to me, and I to the world. For I bear on my body the marks of Jesus" (Gal. 6:14,17).

WEEK SIX ✤ SAFE IN HIS EMBRACE

That's all you've got left. Die to everything else.

And how about that big brother at your Father's house? He's pretty scary, isn't he? You may not realize it, but he's going to be one of the biggest obstacles Satan is going to use to keep you from returning home with your whole heart.

He may eye you. He may judge you. He may resent like crazy any hint that God may choose to use you. Oh, he is powerful. But he is not your Father, and he is not in charge.

Don't get the wrong idea. The Father loves him every bit as much as He loves you, but if big brother doesn't get that chip off his shoulder, he may find himself out in the woodshed with Dad. Oh, what he misses when he won't go to the party!

I hope never again to be a prodigal, but I surely do hope I get an invitation to many a prodigal's homecoming dance. It's pride that can't celebrate with a prodigal-come-home. Folks who won't come are still kidding themselves into thinking they did something right to be loved by their Father.

Not all big brothers are Pharisees, but I can't help reflecting on that parable in Luke 18:9-14. Read it one last time. How did the tax collector go home according to verse 14?

_____

_____

Justified. That's a huge word. If the truth be known, we don't really like God's rules. They minimize our egos. And until we are crucified, we are nothing but walking egos.

We desperately want to have something to do with our justification. We spend untold energies trying to justify ourselves. Oh, what freedom to give up! Plunder your disaster until you find the crown jewel of unjustifiable justification!

Big brother won't mind if you come back as long as you hang your head and wear your shame. But when God has the audacity to give you a little dignity back and you dare lift your radiant face to heaven in liberated praise, big brother may be appalled!

Read Romans 8:28-34. Who is the One who justifies?

_____

God may use men to guide the prodigal home, to teach the prodigal how to stay in his own yard, and even help discipline the prodigal, ... but it is God who justifies. He does it by applying the ransom of your biggest Brother's death to your account.

Had, you don't ever have to apologize that God has forgiven you and has loved you enough to accept you without question and restore you. If you surrender all you've been through to His purposes, you don't have to apologize if He uses your disaster for your good. You don't even have to apologize if He dares to use you shamelessly after what you have done.

If you really learned your lesson, you're not likely ever to be anything but profoundly humbled again, but humility before God and others doesn't mean apologizing for God's embarrassing shows of affection to you.

Face it! God's love for us is scandalous! I look at the words of Philippians 2:7. They say that Christ "made himself of no reputation" (KJV), and I think, *That Christ would dare use someone like me proves that He didn't care much about His reputation!*

Folks who won't come to the party kid themselves that they did something to be loved by their Father.

God has mercy on all who truly repent.

What is God asking of us? Unabashed, unhindered, completely abandoned repentance! No faking. No hedging. No blaming. No excuses. Just "Have mercy on me, a sinner!" That's what He wants out of all of us!

Thankfully, God even has mercy on the self-righteous Pharisee who repents. After all God has done for me, to withhold from the Pharisee the right to splash in the river of forgiveness would make me a bigger hypocrite than he. If we have come to this point in our journey and we still have a shred of self-righteousness left, we are still kidding ourselves about our sin. We are still a great distance from home. To the glory of God, we can still get there, but not without stopping in the valley of repentance and stooping to observe our own reflection in the pond.

Had, all God wants out of us when we come home is repentance and humility. Those two things are so foreign to our human, self-deprecating little-man syndrome that God thinks they're worth celebrating every time He sees them. Frankly, they make God want to party.

Do you remember the part of the prodigal parable when music and dancing echoed all over the countryside? I have always found the terminology of David intriguing when he cried out in repentance after his heinous sins, "Make me to hear joy and gladness; that the bones which thou hast broken may rejoice" (Ps. 51:8, KJV).

David had been a true lover of God. He had known glorious intimacy with a heavenly Father whose glory he had seen and words he had heard. He was the very one who penned the words, "Know that the LORD has set apart the godly for himself; the LORD will hear when I call to him" (Ps. 4:3). But he may not have known way back then that the Lord also hears when the ungodly call to him.

In Psalm 51, David was a man stricken by the grief of his own sin. A godly man who turned from the path and foolishly did ungodly things. He was seduced not by a woman but by a powerful unseen force. He denied responsibility for his sins and rationalized his behavior for as long as he could. Then he broke. Leave it to David not to be satisfied with a partial restoration.

David had known the sacred romance. I believe he would rather have died than to be forgiven but held at arm's distance from a God of no more chances.

"Make me to hear joy and gladness; that the bones which thou hast broken may rejoice" (v. 8, KJV). Whose joy and gladness did David want to hear? Oh, Beloved, without a doubt it was God's! His Father's! "Abba, my Abba! I can only bear to come home if You are glad to see me! If I could only hear Your joy over my return, these bones that You have broken will rejoice!"

David couldn't have stood it any other way. Line it up beside Jesus' parable of the prodigal, and you find a perfect example why David was a man after God's own heart. If he couldn't return to God's heart, he couldn't bear to return to God's home.

Go back to your Father's heart, not just His home.

Had, you will never be healed any other way. Do not go back to your Father's table to eat the crumbs on the floor like a dog. Think more of His redemption than that. Do not go back to your Father's house just to be safe. He wants far more for you than that. You will never heal if you only go back to your Father's home. You must go back to His heart. Closer than you've ever been.

Ah, there He is just now. Coming across the field. He is running in your direction. He doesn't even see me right now. He only has eyes for you. Forget your speeches. He wants to hug you. He wants to kiss you. Your healing will come in your very own Abba's tight and passionate embrace. Let Him hold you so close that you can hear His heart pounding from having run to you.

Don't stop Him when He wants to put a robe on your back. A ring on your finger. And sandals on your feet. Do not take this moment from Him. Feast on the fatted calf. Then listen as He makes you to hear His joy and gladness. Press your ear to the floor and let your heart be caught in the rhythm of the steps of your Father's dance. Then get up off of that floor and let your broken bones rejoice. That will forever be the most authentic sign of a prodigal's gratitude.

Don't be afraid! He wouldn't run like that if He weren't glad to see you! Look at the way He's springing up that hill! He's yelling something. I can't quite make it out. Oh, now I hear it. He's yelling, "Son!"

That was your name all along! Not Good or Proud.

"Son!"

Farewell, Had.

Write Micah 7:8 below and claim it as your own!

_____

_____

I tricked you into thinking
   I would never be all right.
That's what I thought too.
   I lied.
My God thought differently,
   and I've decided to believe Him
    instead of you.
My enemy,
   You've been Had.

Video Response Sheet
GROUP SESSION 6

The Greek word for "understand" is *suniemi* which means "assembling individual facts into an organized

whole, as collecting the pieces of a puzzle and putting them together."

Any eye that may be willing to be opened, any ear that might be willing to hear, any mind that might

be willing to receive understanding could receive a puzzle piece and know just a measure of healing.

So, Beloved, this is your piece. This is your joy.

1. The sin that is _____ from ours always seems _____.

2. The Word of God _____ teaches us to _____ fellowship with the repentant.

3. We _____ go on in our sin. The Holy Spirit will _____ us.

4. How do we go on from here? We go on _____.

5. A true, _____ Had is so scared of herself that she will never live anywhere but

_____ the _____ of God.

ENDNOTES

Week 1

[1]Steve Gallagher, "Devastated by Internet Porn," 15 December 2000, <http://www.purelifeministries.org/mensarticle1.htm>.

[2]Brendan I. Koerner, "A Lust for Profits," *U.S. News & World Report,* 27 March 2000, <http://www.usnews.com>.

[3]Spiros Zodhiates, ed., *The Complete Word Study Dictionary: New Testament* (Chattanooga, TN: AMG Publishers, 1992), #4301, 1222.

[4]Charles Ryrie, *Basic Theology: A Popular Systematic Guide to Understanding Biblical Truth* (Chicago: Moody, 1999), 192.

Week 2

[1]Spiros Zodhiates, "Lexical Aids to the Old Testament," 8709, in Spiros Zodhiates, Warren Baker, and David Kemp, *The Hebrew-Greek Key Study Bible* (Chattanooga, TN: AMG Publishers, 1996), #8709, 1556.

[2]Ibid., #8706, 1556.

[3]*Practical Word Studies in the New Testament, Vol. 2* (Chattanooga, TN: Leadership Ministries Worldwide, 1998), 1801.

[4]Spiros Zodhiates, ed., *The Complete Word Study New Testament* (Iowa Falls: World Bible Publishers, Inc., 1992), #1180, 47.

[5]Zodhiates, ed., *The Complete Word Study Dictionary: New Testament,* # 3180, 954.

Week 3

[1]Spiros Zodhiates, "Lexical Aids to the New Testament," in Zodhiates, Baker, and Kemp, *The Hebrew-Greek Key Study Bible,* #6038, 1688-89.

Week 4

[1]Spiros Zodhiates, "Lexical Aids to the New Testament," in Zodhiates, Baker, and Kemp, *The Hebrew-Greek Key Study Bible,* #1921, 1621.

[2]*Webster's Ninth New Collegiate Dictionary* (Springfield, MA: Merriam-Webster Inc., 1988), s.v. "messy."

Week 6

[1]Zodhiates, *The Complete Word Study Dictionary: New Testament,* #4893, 1339.

How to Become a Christian

"God so loved the world that he gave his one and only Son, that whoever believes in him shall not perish but have eternal life."

—John 3:16

All have sinned and fall short of the glory of God.

—Romans 3:23

The wages of sin is death, but the gift of God is eternal life in Christ Jesus our Lord.

—Romans 6:23

God demonstrates his own love for us in this: While we were still sinners, Christ died for us!

—Romans 5:8

If you confess with your mouth, "Jesus is Lord," and believe in your heart that God raised him from the dead, you will be saved.

—Romans 10:9

If anyone is in Christ, he is a new creation; the old has gone, the new has come!

—2 Corinthians 5:17

The Bible tells us that God is a God of love. His virtues include kindness, compassion, justice, faithfulness, patience, and truthfulness. But the Bible also tells us that we all fall short of the goodness of God. Although we may do good things, nothing we can do measures up to His standard of righteousness. We all deserve to be punished.

God's remedy for this impossible situation was to send His Son Jesus to be our substitute, bearing the penalty for evil in our place. Jesus Christ's death on the cross was a gift of love from God the Father. Accepting Jesus' death as payment for our sin is the only way we can meet God's standard. When we accept Christ's sacrifice, God the Father accepts and adopts us as His children.

If you are willing to confess that you are a sinner, that you want to turn from your sin in repentance and invite Jesus to be your Savior and Lord of your life, pray this simple prayer:

Dear God, I know I have sinned by breaking your laws. I ask for your forgiveness. I believe Jesus died for my sins. I want to receive Him as my Savior and Lord. I want to obey Him in all that I do. In the name of Jesus I pray. Amen.

Entering into a relationship with Jesus not only makes Him our Savior from our sins but also acknowledges Him as Lord of our lives. Now Jesus sits on the throne of our lives and deserves the right to rule our hearts through and through. We now have a new nature.

Unfortunately, this new nature competes with the old nature of sin. Fortunately, God also gives us His gift of the Holy Spirit. As we cooperate with His Spirit, He transforms us from the inside out for the rest of our lives. Becoming more like Jesus is a process that involves Bible study, prayer, and being a member of a church.

If you prayed the prayer to receive Jesus as Savior and Lord, contact your small group leader, your pastor, or a trusted Christian friend and tell them of your decision. They would be happy to pray with you. If you are not confident that you are a Christian, take the same steps. This decision is too important to leave undecided. May God bless you.

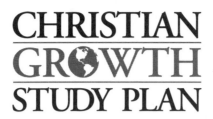

CHRISTIAN GROWTH STUDY PLAN

In the **Christian Growth Study Plan (formerly Church Study Course)**, this book *When Godly People Do Ungodly Things* is a resource for course credit in the subject area Personal Life of the Christian Growth category of plans. To receive credit, read the book, complete the learning activities, show your work to your pastor, a staff member or church leader, then complete the following information. This page may be duplicated. Send the completed page to:

Christian Growth Study Plan
One LifeWay Plaza, Nashville, TN 37234-0117
FAX: (615)251-5067, Email: *cgspnet@lifeway.com*
For information about the Christian Growth Plan, refer to the Christian Growth Study Plan Catalog. It is located online at *www.lifeway.com/cgsp*. If you do not have access to the Internet, contact the Christian Growth Study Plan office (1.800.968.5519) for the specific plan you need for your ministry.

WHEN GODLY PEOPLE DO UNGODLY THINGS
COURSE NUMBER: CG-0822

PARTICIPANT INFORMATION

Social Security Number (USA ONLY-optional)	Personal CGSP Number*	Date of Birth (MONTH, DAY, YEAR)

Name (First, Middle, Last)		Home Phone

Address (Street, Route, or P.O. Box)	City, State, or Province	Zip/Postal Code

Please check appropriate box: ❑ Resource purchased by self ❑ Resource purchased by church ❑ Other

CHURCH INFORMATION

Church Name

Address (Street, Route, or P.O. Box)	City, State, or Province	Zip/Postal Code

CHANGE REQUEST ONLY

☐ Former Name

☐ Former Address	City, State, or Province	Zip/Postal Code

☐ Former Church	City, State, or Province	Zip/Postal Code

Signature of Pastor, Conference Leader, or Other Church Leader	Date

*New participants are requested but not required to give SS# and date of birth. Existing participants, please give CGSP# when using SS# for the first time. Thereafter, only one ID# is required. **Mail to:** Christian Growth Study Plan, One LifeWay Plaza, Nashville, TN 37234-0117. Fax: (615)251-5067.

Rev. 3-03

LOOK FOR THESE OTHER GREAT BOOKS AND JOURNALS FROM BETH MOORE

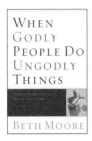

When Godly People Do Ungodly Things
Hardcover, 0-8054-2465-2

Beth Moore confronts the hard questions
of faith and faithfulness, delivering the
dire warnings to Christians to safeguard
themselves against Satan's attacks.

Praying God's Word
Deluxe Bonded Leather Edition
0-8054-2760-0

To be set free from strongolds which claim our lives,
we have to replace them with the mind of Christ and
fervent daily prayer. *Praying God's Word*, Leather
Gift Edition, is a topical prayer guide addressing 14
strongholds and what Scripture reveals about each.
Also available:
Hardcover: 0-8054-2351-6
Devotional Journal: 0-8054-3790-8

A Heart Like His
Hardcover, 0-8054-2035-5

This book guides readers on an exciting a
informative journey through twists and turn
David's life. Learn how to better serve Go
understanding your unique relationship to
Also Available:
Devotional Journal: 0-8054-3528-X

Jesus the One and Only
Hardcover, 0-8054-2489-X

In *Jesus the One and Only,* Beth introduces you
to the Savior and with an up close and personal
portrait of His life. God uses Beth's words to
woo you into a romance with the One and Only.

To Live Is Christ
Hardcover, 0-8054-2423-7

This book takes you on a spiritual odyssey
through the life of the apostle Paul, one of the
New Testament's most prominent characters.

Breaking Free
Hardcover, 0-8054-2294-3

Selected passages from the Book of Isai
draw parallels between the captive Israel
and today's Christian to show how to
make freedom in Christ a daily reality.

Things Pondered
Hardcover, 0-8054-0166-0

Celebrate the treasured moments in life as told
through a collection of remembrances of children,
Christmas, marriage, trials, friendship, the seasons,
grace, and—above all—God's love.

BROADMAN
&HOLMAN
PUBLISHERS

Feathers from My Nest
Hardcover, 0-8054-2464-4

A sentimental blend of a mother's rich
memories with solid spiritual applicati
as only Beth Moore could do.